THE THIRD LIE

DEDICATION

For Judy, who always believed in this book

THE THIRD LIE

Why Government Programs Don't Work—And a Blueprint for Change

Richard J. Gelles

Walnut Creek, California

LEFT COAST PRESS, INC.
1630 North Main Street, #400
Walnut Creek, CA 94596
http://www.LCoastPress.com

ISBN 978-1-61132-050-3 hardcover
ISBN 978-1-61132-051-0 paperback
ISBN 978-1-61132-052-7 electronic

Library of Congress Cataloging-in-Publication Data

Gelles, Richard J.
The third lie : why government programs don't work—and a blueprint for change / Richard J. Gelles.
    p. cm.
    Includes bibliographical references and index.
    ISBN 978-1-61132-050-3 (hardback : alk. paper) — ISBN 978-1-61132-051-0 (pbk. : alk. paper) — ISBN 978-1-61132-052-7 (ebook)
1. United States—Social policy—1993- 2. Health care reform—United States. 3. Educational sociology—United States. 4. Public welfare—United States. 5. Middle class—United States—Economic conditions—21st century. I. Title.
    HN65.G44 2011
    320.60973'09049—dc23
                2011026448

Printed in the United States of America

⊚™ The paper used in this publication meets the minimum requirements of American National Standard for Information Sciences—Permanence of Paper for Printed Library Materials, ANSI/NISO Z39.48–1992.

CONTENTS

Acknowledgments

Of all my books, this one took the longest to write and traveled the most winding road. Through all the drafts and revisions, my strongest supporter and motivator was my wife, Judy. Without her pushing and rereading of drafts, the manuscript would still be in a drawer in my office. And, again, unlike any other book I have ever written, I sought more advice and feedback from my colleagues than ever before. Without a push from Ram Cnaan, the four draft chapters would have been the end of my efforts. My colleagues at the School of Social Policy & Practice provided me pointed and helpful reactions when I presented the main argument of the book at a school colloquium. Staci Perlman, Cassie Bevan, and Cindy Geeslin read at least one draft of the manuscript and helped me sharpen my prose and arguments. Richard Barth and Michael Sherraden gave me constructive criticism. My assistant, Laura Nickrosz, read the final three drafts and helped me dig out the remaining spelling and grammatical errors. Laura also kept everyone at bay while I worked on the final drafts of the manuscript.

It took a significant team effort at the end to complete this project. I sent out a call for assistance to Jo Ann Miller who was my editor for *The Book of David: How Preserving Families Can Cost Children's Lives*. Joanne is a fabulous editor who was invaluable in putting together the final structure and tone of the book. Roberto de Viqc de Crumptich designed such a great cover for *The Book of David* that I recruited him to create the cover for this book. He truly captured the spirit of the manuscript and offered me far too many wonderful options for the cover. The final key player in the production team was my friend, former editor, and current publisher Mitch Allen. Thanks, Mitch.

Introduction

GOVERNMENT PROGRAMS: THE GOOD, THE BAD, AND THE UGLY

As the old joke says, there are three big lies: first, "Of course I will respect you in the morning"; second, "The check is in the mail"; and third, "I am from the government, and I am here to help you." This book is about the third lie.

It's a simple task to review government social programs and demonstrate the failure of good intentions because, as the third lie suggests, the argument is delivered to an accepting audience. For the public and much of the media, waste and fraud in government programs are givens. Well-drawn portraits of welfare queens, freeloaders, and corrupt and wasteful administrators are widely disseminated. Virtually every political candidate for a federal office either attacks waste and fraud or uses presumed waste and fraud as the basis for proposing a new and better program (which, of course, will not be fraught with waste and fraud).

The belief that government programs do not and cannot work is one of many factors underscoring the ferocity of opposition to the Obama administration's proposals for financial and health care reform. The very existence of the Tea Party and their anti-incumbent campaigns demonstrates that a large audience subscribes to the notion of government incompetence.

Before the economic crisis of 2008, a sardonic excoriation of the failure of government programs would have been merely amusing. But as I write this, in early 2011, government's inability to provide genuine help for serious social problems is a crisis and a tragedy. From when the mortgage default and bankruptcies of large investment banks such as Lehman Brothers began in the fall of 2008 until the midterm election in November 2010, the federal government has spent and invested hundreds of billions of dollars to prop up failing financial institutions and stimulate a depressed economy. And yet the economy is still balky; the unemployment rate is near 10 percent nationally and above 12 percent in some states. The middle class, if there still is one, has slowed down its spending. Housing sales are increasing, but at a much slower rate than one would expect, given that home mortgage rates are the lowest they have ever been in modern times. The stock market may have exceeded 12,000 in February 2011, but that still has not helped the broad middle class. A second and profound government shortcoming, mostly at the state and local level, is in education. The graduation rate for inner-city minority youth is under 50 percent in many large urban areas, low enough to generate the dismal prediction that youngsters who do not graduate high school are likely to live a life as have-nots and never-will-haves. This population may be unreachable by even the most effective (albeit rare) government programs.

But the facts about the government's inability to help and the plausible solutions that could work are hardly simple. I am a social scientist, researcher, and presently dean of the School of Social Policy & Practice at the University of Pennsylvania. In the last ten years, I have undertaken the task of slogging through the murk and morass of government efforts. My first goal was to explain why existing programs live up to the third lie. Next, I sought out those programs that seemed to work—even if they were not perfect. I analyzed those that showed evidence of being effective, assessed the quality of the evidence, and drew out the commonalities between the effective programs. Last, and most important, I synthesized what I learned about the "bad" and the "ugly" programs as well as the "good" and effective efforts, and developed my own policy that would have a good chance of being successful, of actually helping people.

The task of separating the good from the bad and ugly is complex for at least four reasons. First, most people believe "I'm from the government and I am here to help you" is just a big lie. Second, those on the right want no part of more big government and more spending. Third, those on the left continue to believe that more and more funding for bigger and bigger programs is the answer, despite a good deal of evidence to the contrary. Fourth, any program will have to meet the daunting challenge of being truly affordable, with a funding formula that is not merely smoke and mirrors.

I believe that the key to success for any government effort is the support of a vital, vibrant middle class. The current economic crisis persists because what is left of the middle class is afraid to spend, afraid to invest, and afraid to be only a step away from poverty. To succeed, government policy must address this reality.

Chapter 1

THERE OUGHT TO BE A LAW!

In 1977, I had just become chair of the Department of Sociology and Anthropology at the University of Rhode Island. I was thirty-one years old and had the temperament typical of social reformers. My professional focus was the study of child abuse and violence against women, and so by profession and specialty I was already an advocate for the oppressed and disadvantaged.

The department's offices were on the first and fifth floors of a five-year-old building, the Chafee Social Science Center (named after the former governor and then junior senator from Rhode Island, John Chafee). Legend had it that the Chafee building, with its eight-story office tower, was the tallest building between Providence and New Haven. The tower had two elevators, which had already become the butt of "lowest bidder" jokes because of the cranky functioning and frequent breakdowns. Nonetheless, even those of us who were relatively fit eventually came to use the elevators to go between the offices on the first and fifth floors.

One afternoon, I got on the elevator to go to the fifth floor with a young woman, whom those days before political correctness I would have called a dwarf (now she might be called a "little person"). It immediately became obvious to both of us that she had a problem. The buttons for each floor were positioned vertically on the elevator wall, and she could only reach the button for the second floor. This was a serious inconvenience, since, as she told me, she was headed to the Economics Department on the eighth floor. I pushed the "8" button for her and we began to go up.

In the few moments it took us to reach the fifth floor, it became clear there was a significant obstacle to her education. How, she asked me, could she major in economics if she could not even get to the department office? Walking up eight flights every day would be out of the question.

In my best "champion of the oppressed" voice, I asked her to come to my office and let me help her. There, I quickly called a colleague who worked for the vice president for Student Affairs and asked if she could meet with the woman and help her resolve the problem. My colleague agreed, and I sent the young woman off. When she left, I sat back and grinned smugly, congratulating myself on my gallant act of social justice. I had advocated for an "oppressed" person who had a "personal problem," and I assumed all would be right in the world.

My smugness lasted less than an hour. The young woman came back, and when she arrived at my door, I assumed she was there to thank me. But instead she had come to tell me what a futile runaround she experienced. The vice president for Student Affairs sent her to the person responsible for students with learning disabilities (per the provisions of the Rehabilitation Act of 1973, PL 93-112). The university, because it received federal funds, had set up an office for disabled students. But the head of the Office of Student Disabilities said she was only able to deal with learning disabilities and really could not suggest a solution.

The woman in charge of the Office of Student Disabilities then called the facilities office, which suggested that the young woman purchase a television antenna and carry it in her purse. She could telescope the antenna to push the "8" button on the Chafee elevator. I actually thought that suggestion was reasonably creative and better than putting a footstool in each elevator.

However, the student was neither amused nor empowered by her travels through the university bureaucracy. She was angry that no one seemed to take her problem seriously and realize that her elevator troubles went beyond the problem of getting to the eighth floor. What she had discovered was that the university was simply neither physically nor bureaucratically equipped to accommodate her personal situation.

For what sociologists call a "personal trouble"[1] to become a social issue, it has to capture the public's attention, generate public concern and controversy, and produce collective action. The demand for change typically occurs when people view a situation as wrong and feel that *rights* have been violated. The young woman wanted a college education at a state-supported institution and wanted to major in economics. She was blocked because of a decision to install buttons vertically in an elevator. A person in a wheelchair would have also been unable to push the "8" button.

Problems like this are injustices, not merely misfortunes. Thus, when injustices are perceived, there is an effort to bring attention to them and seek a resolution. The rallying cry is often, "There ought to be a law!"

As famously expressed by the late Speaker of the House, Tip O'Neill, and often repeated, "All politics is local." That claim notwithstanding, many complaints about the ineffectiveness of government focus on the federal level. Granted, many state and local policies address personal troubles and social issues. But the wholesale delivery of government assistance in the form of sweeping policies—not to mention the deepest well of funding—exists at the federal level. Even though constrained by the Constitution not to become involved in matters that are the province of the states, the federal government is identified by the provisions of that same Constitution as the ultimate protector of human rights and the ultimate source of redress of personal injustice. The road to good intentions most often starts in Washington because Washington has the deepest pockets and the biggest stick—the U.S. Constitution.

POLICY, LAW, AND RESIDUAL SOCIAL POLICIES

Cries that "there ought to be a law!" are typically grounded in the plight of one individual or a group of individuals who have experienced injustice. When physician C. Henry Kempe began to see children admitted to the Colorado General Hospital with fractures and injuries that could only have been inflicted by a caregiver, he was appalled by the medical profession's lack of response to these injuries. Why weren't physicians and nurses recognizing them as deliberate attacks on the children? How many such injuries occurred each year and how many were ignored or overlooked by physicians, nurses, teachers, counselors, social workers, and others in the helping professions?

Kempe's contribution to the field of child welfare was that first he turned a "personal trouble" into a call-to-arms for the medical community to view physical child abuse as a social issue; and then he championed mandatory reporting laws. His goal was to generate collective action to remedy the problem of intentional injury of children. Without the law, Kempe's research, his articles in the medical journals, and his social advocacy would have produced only minimal social change.

There are many similar stories about personal troubles that led to collective action and ultimately a law. In 1981 John Walsh, when his son Adam was kidnapped and killed, turned his own tragedy into a social issue that led to federal legislation on missing and exploited children. Another social injustice, wife abuse, had been part of the fabric of American families since the seventeenth century. Efforts to address it had waxed and waned for decades. There had been some state legislation, but it was only after the O.J. Simpson case that this kind of crime gained federal attention. When the case burst into the headlines in 1994, Congress quickly enacted the first version of the Violence Against Women Act. When the bill was up for reauthorization in 1996, one of the lead witnesses before the Senate Judiciary Committee was Denise Brown, sister of the slain Nicole Brown Simpson.

The grounding in personal tragedy of calls for social action tends to produce a particular type of policy. There are two main government approaches in the area of social policy and social welfare. The first, and most widely used, is what scholars Neil Gilbert and Paul Terrell call the "residual model."[2] This model, which others refer to as "targeted social programs," evolved in the United States in the 1930s in response to the Great Depression. According to Gilbert and Terrell, a "residual model" arises when existing institutions—family, education, the economy—fail to meet individual and family needs. Residual policies are created on the assumption that, although our political, social, and economic institutions generally operate effectively and meet most of the population's needs, some problems remain that require targeted or residual social policies.[3] The "residual model" is a temporary (although it might ultimately become permanent) safety net created by the government. Those who support this model believe government should be small, decentralized, and respond only when absolutely necessary.

In the United States today there is a long list of residual social welfare policies. Federal and state child maltreatment policies, including mandatory reporting laws, respond to residual cases in which parents cannot or will not protect and care for their children. Domestic violence legislation is aimed at the residual families and couples in which the conflict rises to the level of physical and sexual violence. The core residual policies for domestic violence consist in using the criminal justice system, in the form of restraining orders, arrests, prosecutions, and court-ordered counseling, to protect victims and prevent future violence.

Supplemental Social Security (SSI) provides financial resources to older people whose Social Security benefits are insufficient to meet some basic needs. Aid to Families with Dependent Children (AFDC) was the core welfare residual policy until 1996, when the policy became even more residual—as captured by the new title, Temporary Assistance to Needy Families (TANF). And last—but for the purposes of this book, not least—the Americans with Disabilities Act (ADA) and the Individuals with Educational Disabilities Act (IDEA) are residual policies for children whose learning, physical, or mental health disabilities or challenges produce special needs requiring accommodation by schools.

The second government approach, "the institutional model," views social welfare as a set of permanent and centralized institutions that serve a preventative function. The "institutional model" is not a safety net, does not specifically target programs and services, and does not have a "means test" nor requires a shortcoming or disability to qualify for services and support.[4]

The best example of an institutional social policy is the Social Security program. The key assumption behind Social Security is that the elderly, having retired, need an assured income. This is accomplished by taxing the working population and paying benefits to everyone after a certain age. Currently, people born before 1937 may receive full benefits at age sixty-five; they may receive partial benefits at age sixty-two. Eligibility age for full benefits is higher for those born after 1937—so for baby boomers born in 1946 the age for full benefits is sixty-six. Of course, Social Security benefits are not really universal, since one has to work forty quarters (three months) in order to qualify for them. However, Social Security is obviously universal in that people receive benefits irrespective of whether they have no assets or billions in assets. I will have more to say about the current state and solvency of Social Security in Chapter 3.

FEDERALISM AND SOCIAL POLICY

Most government social policies are residual. The rationale for this is grounded in the Constitution. The United States operates under the governmental principle of federalism. It would be too much of a digression to go through the history and philosophy of federalism and the debates about it that have raged for more than two hundred years. At the core of the issue is the fact that the founders of the United States and the authors of the Constitution set out to create a republic with a relatively weak central government. The federal government is vested by the Constitution with the power to tax, provide for the common defense and general welfare of the nation, borrow money, regulate interstate commerce, manage immigration, coin and print money, set standards for weights and measures, establish post offices, issue patents and copyrights, establish courts, declare war, raise and support a military, and support civil rights. This seems like a long list, but it is actually quite limited. Everything else, all other regulations and policies, are left to the states.

The federal government does not directly run public education. It does not directly provide intervention and treatment for victims of child abuse. It does not provide direct social services for victims of domestic violence. It does assist the needy through residual social policies, including welfare, food stamps (now called SNAP—Supplemental Food and Nutrition Program), the earned income tax credit (EITC), and Medicaid.

These are classic residual means-tested programs. Only those who "need" the assistance are eligible to receive the services.

In reality, when it comes to dealing with personal troubles and social issues, the federal government is relatively weak. By weak, I do not mean powerless. Rather, I mean it is hard for the federal government to enact legislation that gives it a direct role in helping. The prolonged debate over health care reform—which ended in a larger role for the federal government—is a prime example of how difficult it is to enact big "helping" legislation.

This was exactly what the founders wanted. They established a system of checks and balances—the executive branch, the legislative branch, and the judiciary—and then limited the actual powers of the central government. The working of the federal government, with legislation moving through the House of Representatives and the Senate, the veto power of the President, and the constitutional oversight of the Supreme Court, further limits federal power. There are more than five hundred legislators in both branches of the Congress, thousands of staff, and yet, on average, only one hundred pieces of legislation are passed each year (not counting resolutions and the naming of post offices). This is not a function of a tangled and gridlocked political bureaucracy; this was the intent of the founders.

The fabric of the federal government created by the Constitution makes it difficult to enact legislation. As former Senate Majority Leader George Mitchell said to the graduating class of the Senate Page School in 1994, "The Founders wanted to make it hard for Congress to *do something bad,* thus legislators are constrained in doing good things as well." This structure seems to have served the nation well for more than two hundred years. Federalism does put severe limits on federal social policy—it constrains the ability of the federal government to establish institutional social policies as well as enact residual solutions. But even when government comes together to enact social policies—and this is especially true with residual or targeted social programs—the intended and unintended consequences of residual policies provide ample anecdotal evidence of the third lie.

RESIDUAL POLICIES, ELIGIBILITY, AND OPEN-ENDED ENTITLEMENTS

Hawaii and the Individuals with Disabilities Education Act

As I will discuss in greater detail in Chapter 2, in 1993, in Hawaii, a group of parents of disabled children filed a class-action lawsuit against the state. The parents obtained legal counsel and filed suit in federal court against Hawaii, arguing that the schools of the state of Hawaii had violated their children's civil rights guaranteed by the Fourteenth Amendment. The basis of the parents' claim was that Hawaii was out of compliance with Section 504 of the Individuals with Disabilities Education Act of 1993 (IDEA) and had been out of compliance for twenty years.[5] The suit itself was not unique—similar suits had been filed against school districts on the mainland over the previous thirty years. When the suit was settled in 1994, the consent decree stipulated the definition by which children were in the so-called "Felix class," named for Jennifer Felix, one of the plaintiffs in the suit. The definition was (and is): "The 'Plaintiff class' is all children and adolescents with disabilities residing in Hawaii, from birth to twenty years of age, who are eligible for and in need of educational and mental health services." This definition drew from the stipulations of the federal Individuals with Disabilities Education Act[6] and Section 504 of the Rehabilitation Act of 1973.[7] The exact wording is included in the footnotes.

The relevant issues are found in and between the lines. In the lines of IDEA is the specific statement that "the term 'child with a disability' [...] may, at the discretion of the state and the local educational agency, include a child..." Thus, the federal statute gives to the states and local educational agencies the discretion to define operationally what is meant by a disability. Said another way, the states have the authority to determine who is eligible for disability services or who will be "targeted" for the services.

Between the lines of both the IDEA and Section 504 of the Rehabilitation Act of 1973, it is clear that federal lawmakers meant to provide only a broad definition of the term "disability." In keeping with federalism, the framers of federal residual policies give states latitude and discretion to determine eligibility. When disputes occur, as they almost always do with residual policies that have broad definitions, they are often arbitrated in a federal court, as in the Felix case.

The federal government provided only the broadest definition of which children might be eligible for special education and mental health services under the provisions of federal education. The consent decree that resulted from the *Felix v. Waihee* federal suit used a similar broad definition as to which children were included in the Felix class and thus were eligible for services under the terms of the consent decree. It was left to the local educational agencies and the individual school complexes to make the actual decisions regarding which children were in or out of the class. In practice, these decisions would be made as part of each student's Individual Educational Plan (IEP), a process also required under the terms of IDEA. In Hawaii, if there was a disagreement regarding the

IEP decision, the parents could bring the case to a due process hearing[8] for a resolution of the dispute.

What resulted from the Felix consent decree is a template for what can occur when the federal government creates a new residual entitlement and provides only the most general guidelines for who is eligible. Here is a stark example of how good intentions and a law can go in the wrong direction.

In 1994, when the Felix consent decree was signed by both parties and affirmed by the judge, there were 2,894 children in the state of Hawaii who were, as a result of IEP evaluations, included in the Felix class. That same year, the Hawaii Department of Education's expenses for special education totaled $24.5 million. The Hawaii Department of Health's budget for Felix-class children was $156.4 million, making the state's total Felix-related costs $180 million.

Five years later, in 1999–2000, the Felix class had multiplied four times to 11,842 children. By 2000, the Department of Education's Felix budget was $109 million, the Department of Health's was up to $192 million, and the total was $301 million. And the state had not reached compliance with the consent decree. With the deadlines for compliance looming in 2001 and then pushed back to 2002, DOE's budget was up to $179 million; DOH was getting $148 million, for a total of $327 million. This figure was lower than the $400 million that had been the two agencies' original request. The final seven-year total Felix-related expenditures were just under $1.5 billion—and the state was still not in compliance! In the space of seven years, Hawaii went from a limited, relatively stingy approach to the needs of disabled children to an approach that funded almost every request.

How could the number of children eligible for special education and mental health services grow so rapidly? How could a well-meaning residual educational policy grow to outspend the entire state's general revenue allocation for higher education? There are a number of answers, ranging from benign and well-meaning to what I consider to be *the core flaw of government residual social policies.*

The well-meaning explanation is simple: the growth of the Felix-class population simply reflects the educational agencies doing a much better job of identifying children with special education and mental health needs. The stick of having to comply with a federal consent decree and the additional state funding from the Department of Education and the Department of Health allowed schools and mental health agencies to offer vastly improved diagnostic services. Parents now brought their children forward for diagnoses, plans, and programs. This explanation supports the basic principle and intent of residual social programs.

A less well-meaning explanation is that the consent decree and mandate to provide services motivated schools and IEP teams to err on the side of applying a disability diagnosis even when there was doubt about the child's problem. Whereas the state education and health departments and legislature had taken a stingy approach before, the assumption was now that they would fund almost anything to get out from under the control of the federal court. Given that schools were offering more services and the state was required to provide those services, there was an incentive to be inclusive rather than exclusive when evaluating a child.

It is important to keep in mind, though, that the services came with a pejorative label: physical or mental "disability." No matter what politically correct term one uses, the label was not going to be "normal" or "gifted." In educational settings, "special" does not mean good. Some parents and children accepted the label as the price for services. Other parents may have even sought the label because they believed the Felix-class children were getting better educational services than non-Felix children. But another group of parents, including many Hawaiian or Asian parents, refused to accept the IEP diagnosis and responded to the diagnosis by saying "my child is not mental." Thus, a generous diagnostic process could still produce resistance.

Moving along the continuum from more to less benign explanations, a third possibility is that the Felix case offered the local mental health agencies a new and seemingly limitless revenue stream. School IEPs had to include psychologists for testing and diagnosis—the results of which determined whether a child would reach a clinical threshold for a mental health issue or special education. The particular diagnosis would then determine what services would be offered.

A few more facts are needed to complete the picture. First, as may already be obvious, the Hawaii special education and mental health systems were woefully underfunded prior to *Felix v. Waihee*. Second, Hawaii was in the midst of a continuing recession, which also limited the cash flow to community mental health agencies and human service providers. Last, managed care and decades of decreasing federal support for social services further eroded the economic base.

With the Felix consent decree, psychologists became the critical gatekeepers to determine eligibility for state-funded mental health and social services. Once included in the Felix class, children would have to receive services, and those services would most likely be provided by community mental health and social service agencies. (In 1994, the Department of Health's budget for Felix-related cases was six times greater than that of the Department of Education.) It would not take too long for a psychologist to determine that each child he or she diagnosed as belonging in the Felix class would then receive services from the psychologist or the psychologist's agency. The more open the gate, the larger the number of cases, and the greater the revenue.

Even if one opts for the most benign and altruistic explanation for the growth of the Felix class and the ensuing geometric increase in cost, it is clear that there is an inherent and fatal flaw in well-meaning federal residual social policies. That flaw is that the federal government creates an entitlement to resolve a social problem and then provides only a general framework to determine who is covered by the entitlement—leaving the details of the definition to the state.

Various forces work to pry open the gates with regard to eligibility, and before long, the residual policy becomes a gusher of spending and a virtual open-ended entitlement. Neither the federal government nor the state anticipates this growth, and they soon find that they have to fund the skyrocketing cost increases. As a consequence, states begin to siphon money off other programming. Thus, in Hawaii, school spending shifted from general spending to covering Felix-class costs. Some astute parents recognized this and fought to have their children included in the Felix class, thus spawning even more growth and more cost.

The vicious circle of residual policy eligibility is not unique to special education or mental health. It is endemic to many of the best-intentioned residual government social programs. The problem of abused and neglected children provides another stark example.

Child Maltreatment

If a picture is worth a thousand words, a graph may be worth about two hundred. Figure 1 presents the partial story of how child maltreatment was transformed from a personal tragedy, thought to affect fifty thousand or so children, to a social issue and finally a social problem that generated nearly three million reports of child abuse by 2000.

Until the 1960s, there were no laws that required professionals to report suspected cases of child abuse and neglect. Thus, national statistics were essentially non-existent. David Gil, a professor of social welfare at Brandeis University, was the first social scientist who tried to assess the extent of child abuse. In 1967, he conducted a national inventory of reports of child abuse and determined that there were six thousand confirmed cases.[9] At the same time that Gil was conducting his survey, the physician C. Henry Kempe was campaigning to have mandatory reporting laws enacted throughout the United States. The Children's Bureau,

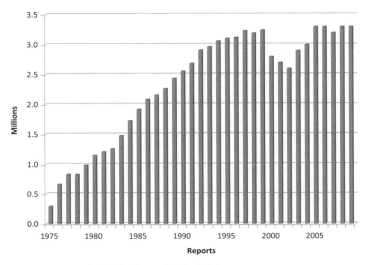

Figure 1. Reports of Child Abuse 1975–2009.

an agency within the then U.S. Department of Health, Education, and Welfare (the precursor to the U.S. Department of Health and Human Services), had developed a model reporting law. By the end of the 1960s, every state had some form of mandatory reporting law. The federal Child Abuse Prevention and Treatment Act (CAPTA) of 1974 attempted to standardize those laws by offering funds to states whose reporting laws conformed to the CAPTA stipulations.

Obviously, reports of child abuse and neglect could be expected to increase once mandatory reporting laws were enacted and standardized at the state level. Figure 1 depicts a rapid increase in reporting after CAPTA was enacted in 1974. The rate of increase slowed a bit in the late 1970s and then accelerated during the 1980s. What happened during that decade is at the core of this discussion.

Returning to the beginning of the 1960s for a moment, it is important to examine the individual tragedies and the social problem that concerned physician Henry Kempe and other activists. In his 1962 article "The Battered Child Syndrome," published in the prestigious *Journal of the American Medical Association,* Kempe defined child abuse as "deliberate acts of physical violence that produce diagnosable injuries."[10] He and his colleagues were concerned with a relatively narrow phenomenon in which parents physically injured their children. The article itself included case examples and X-rays designed to help physicians differentially diagnose inflicted injury.

By 1974, the definition of child abuse and neglect had blossomed to include neglect, emotional abuse, and sexual abuse. Kempe's narrow definition of the battered child syndrome became the following, as stated in CAPTA:

> ...the physical or mental injury, sexual abuse, negligent treatment, or maltreatment of a child under the age of eighteen by a person who is responsible for the child's welfare under circumstances which indicate that the child's welfare is harmed or threatened thereby. (Public Law 93-237)

There was nothing sinister about the expansion of the definition. The definition expanded as well-meaning physicians, social workers, human service workers, and policymakers attempted to ensure that the residual policy covered the full population that required the services and resources granted by the law. The by-products of this well-meaning effort were similar to those of nearly all government residual social policies:

- Resources increase to meet the needs of the growing population included in the broad definition provided in the residual policy.
- Bureaucracies and personnel expand to meet the needs of the population covered by the residual policy.
- The expanded personnel and bureaucracies are able to identify even more cases, thus creating a cycle of growing caseloads, requests for more financial support, expansion of personnel and bureaucracies, and greater case-detection capability.
- The bureaucracies and personnel, firmly established and funded, advocate for an expansion of the definition for the residual class to be sure that *all those in need* of the residual services receive them.
- The bureaucracies and personnel depend on the caseloads to grow or at least remain high to maintain their level of staffing and financial support.

This series of events produces one of the governing rules of residual policies: *the problem never gets better*—assuming fewer in need constitutes "better." Caseloads either must stay the same or grow in order to justify the residual problem's place on the public agenda. There is simply no incentive to reduce detection or caseloads. Of course, there is nothing necessarily wrong with greater case detection and larger and better organizational efforts. Thus, the growing number of child abuse reports could (and some people would argue, should) be considered a great success of government social policy.

Let us add some layers to Figure 1. Figure 2 represents the "pyramid" of child maltreatment reporting that has been typical in the years

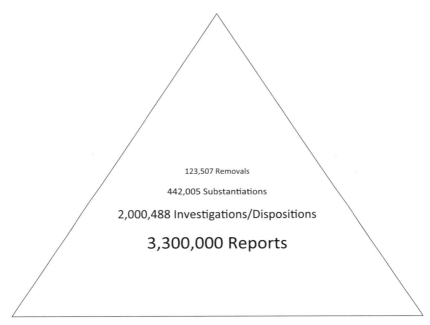

123,507 Removals

442,005 Substantiations

2,000,488 Investigations/Dispositions

3,300,000 Reports

Figure 2. The Child Abuse and Neglect Pyramid.

between 1990 and 2009. In rounded numbers, we typically see that each year about three million children are reported as suspected victims of child maltreatment. Looking back at Figure 1, we see that child-abuse reporting had flattened out by the mid-1990s, suggesting that either most suspected cases of child maltreatment were being reported, or that that child welfare system had reached its full capacity to receive reports. Figure 2 demonstrates that in a typical year, child welfare agencies investigate 60 percent of child maltreatment reports. Thus, the gate is relatively open and the vast majority of child abuse allegations are followed up with some kind of investigation.

The next line shows that upon the completion of investigations, some 22 percent of all investigated reports are substantiated by the child welfare agency. The remaining 78 percent are closed. In some cases families are offered voluntary services, but in most cases their experience with the child welfare system is limited to the investigation.

It would require a long digression to explore in depth the implications of this process. Certainly, some children are, and continue to be, at risk in homes where an investigation shows that the report cannot be substantiated. Reports that are unsubstantiated are not all false reports. And, of course, some cases that are substantiated really do not involve any risk or harm to children.

A second issue is whether there are consequences of an investigation that ends with an "unsubstantiated" finding. For families that have been falsely accused of putting their children at risk, there is the consequence of being unfairly stigmatized. On the other hand, in homes where risk and harm do exist but are undetected, perhaps the mere investigation may deter caregivers from further harmful behavior. There is actually no research on these issues, but they bear mentioning.

Returning to Figure 2, the first line indicates the children who are removed by child welfare services and often the police because of abuse and neglect. This number has been consistently at between 100,000 to 200,000 children each year—some of whom might be removed more than once each year. So what does Figure 2 tell us? That the child welfare system has generated a bureaucracy capable of responding to three million reports of child abuse and neglect in order that 100,000 children a year can be removed from harm's way and an additional 200,000 families can receive social and human services. The most important conclusion is subtler: the child welfare system has invested so much in case detection and investigation that it doesn't have enough personnel and fiscal resources left to offer actual help to children and families in need. As one seasoned child welfare professional concluded, the one, and perhaps only, service the child welfare system offers is an *investigation*. Thus, by investing effort and resources to maximize the residual population of children and families eligible for services, the child welfare system in fact unintentionally reduces the actual help it can provide to those most in need.

Can We Really Target Just Those in Need?

The process by which government becomes involved in helping those in need is both simple and complex. It is simple because, by its nature, the federal government is able to respond to residual social problems. It is complex because the path from personal trouble and injustice to social policy and efforts to help is often indirect, tortuous, and unpredictable. Nonetheless, one thing that is predictable is that once a personal trouble receives the imprimatur of the official government as a legitimate social problem, the definition of the problem will expand, the vagueness of legislative definitions will produce further expansion, and the human service providers who man the frontline gates will expand the problem even more. These bureaucracies, like all bureaucracies, will evolve to be self-sustaining and thus will be best organized to identify more cases and keep the gates open for admission. The growth of the caseload will offer proof that more resources are needed, and so on. Of course, since resources are finite, the investment of resources at the case-detection/ admission level will ultimately dilute the human and fiscal capital available for actual interventions.

One of the most common criticisms of government social programs is that residual programs can evolve into large open-ended entitlements. In Hawaii, the costs associated with complying with the Felix consent decree constituted one-eighth of the Hawaii General Fund Budget in 2001. One-eighth of the state budget went to twelve thousand school-age children who make up 0.009 percent of the state's population.

Attempts to push back on the expansion of eligibility criteria or costs are often met by a response similar to the one Dave and Betsy Cole of East Matunuck, Rhode Island, received from the local school committee. The Coles pointed out to their hometown newspaper, *The Narragansett Times,* that according to the superintendent of schools in South Kingstown, Rhode Island, special education costs were $30,000 per year per student.[11] In all, 20 percent of the students in the system had been identified as needing "special education." Thus, the proportion of the school budget for special education was more than half of the annual school system budget. The Coles went on to argue that receiving a "special education label" was relatively easy, that it was more common when students were in large classes, and that in one family each of the nine children was labeled "special education." The school committee's response to these data was, "It's the law, and there is nothing we can do."

If there is one major reason that government programs so often fail to help, it is the inherent inefficiency and lack of precision of the eligibility gates that form the core component of residual government policies. The welded open eligibility gate and the predictable new costly entitlements undermine the good intentions of the programs by diluting the available resources and diminishing the effectiveness of the proffered assistance.

Chapter 2

WHEN GOOD INTENTIONS GO BAD: THE EDUCATION OF JENNIFER FELIX

J ennifer Felix was born in California in 1973 and was a happy, healthy baby. However, when she was two years old, a viral infection left her brain-damaged, epileptic, and visually and speech impaired. For the first ten years of her life, Jennifer attended a publicly funded special school that provided therapy and counseling for children with emotional and physical problems. In 1983, when Jennifer was ten years old, the family moved to the island of Maui in Hawaii. The special school and special services that were available in California did not exist on Maui. Jennifer's parents' requests and finally demands to the State Department of Education for special education teachers, classroom aids, and therapy went unaddressed. Neither the Department of Education nor the Department of Health had such programs or the funding to launch them. Hawaii has always been a tropical paradise for tourists, but the islands are not rich in social, educational, and mental health resources.

Jennifer attended public school on Maui. The school had no resources to address her special needs, and by her teens Jennifer was self-abusing, had run away from home several times, and was violent toward her mother. Unable to find appropriate services on Maui, Jennifer's mother, Frankie Servetti-Coleman, sent sixteen-year-old Jennifer to the Brown Schools, a residential treatment facility for brain-damaged children in Texas.[1] Jennifer's family paid the cost of transportation and the tuition, and Jennifer finally received the services and therapy she needed.

Frankie Servetti-Coleman's frustrating search for adequate educational services for her daughter was similar to the experiences of thousands of other parents on the islands of Hawaii whose children needed special education and mental health services. The services were not available.

According to Hawaii Department of Education records, there were in 1993 at least two thousand children in Hawaii who had emotional or special education needs. Hawaii had few trained special education teachers and psychologists. The schools did not have funding for case aides who could assist teachers with special-needs children. The community mental health system was equally impoverished—few trained staff and minimal programming for children with special needs.

Nearly every parent who sought help ran into a brick wall. In some cases, such as Jennifer's, the family would use their own financial resources to secure appropriate services. Many other families simply did not have those resources. A third group of families denied that their children even had educational or emotional troubles. Until 1993, each child in Hawaii who had special education or mental health needs was solely a "personal trouble" for the family and teachers. But in 1993, the parents of special-needs children on Hawaii came together to seek redress.

THE INDIVIDUALS WITH DISABILITIES EDUCATION ACT

Fortunately for Frankie Servetti-Coleman and other parents of children on Hawaii with special education needs, Congress had passed the Individuals with Disabilities Education Act (IDEA) in 1973. Section 504 of IDEA requires states to provide children with disabilities a "free and appropriate education," emphasizing the provision of special education and related services to meet the children's unique needs. IDEA and Section 504 grew out of the civil rights movement of the 1960s. Education has generally been envisioned as a civil right, especially after the passage of the Civil Rights Act of 1965. As with race relations, advocates for the educational rights of children with special needs drew upon the equal protection clause of the Fourteenth Amendment of the U.S. Constitution to frame legislation that would ensure that disabled or challenged children would have an equal right to a free and appropriate public education.

Based on the twenty-year-old IDEA, Frankie Servetti-Coleman and other parents realized that Hawaii was out of compliance with the provisions of Section 504. They obtained legal counsel and filed suit in federal court against the state of Hawaii, arguing that their children's civil rights, guaranteed by the Fourteenth Amendment, had been violated by the schools of the state.

Felix versus Waihee

The case was filed in 1993 in federal court, and Jennifer Felix became the named plaintiff in a class action suit, *Felix v. Waihee* (the then governor of Hawaii). The lead attorneys on the case, Shelby Ann Floyd and Eric Seitz, argued that Hawaii was out of compliance with Section 504 of IDEA and had been out of compliance for twenty years.

The case itself was not unique—similar suits had been filed against school districts on the mainland over the past thirty years. The unique feature was that Hawaii is the only state in the United States to have a single statewide school system. Thus, the named defendant was the state governor. Moreover, it would be state agencies, not local school boards, that would be responding to the suit. The state treasury would be fiscally responsible, as opposed to the cities or towns that fund schools with property tax revenues. Finally, and perhaps obviously, the suit was a legal slam dunk—the evidence overwhelmingly supported the plaintiffs, and the state's only defense was that the federal government had not provided adequate funding to implement the mandates of the federal legislation.

When IDEA was passed in 1973, Congress agreed to provide states with 40 percent of the estimated cost of educating a child with a disability. But by 1993, the federal government was providing only 17 percent.[2] The rest of the financial burden fell on the states and the local school districts—which in Hawaii are one and the same. Whether Congress underestimated the number of disabled school children or the actual cost of providing the services is not important here. In the end, the Hawaii legislature and executive branch had to come up with more than 80 percent of the costs of compliance with the federal law.

In 1994, the federal judge hearing the case, David Ezra, issued a summary judgment in favor of the plaintiffs. With no defense, the state entered into a consent decree with the plaintiffs that stipulated how their complaints would be resolved. Both sides agreed to give the state until June 30, 2000, to meet the conditions of the consent decree.

In the meantime, Judge Ezra appointed a monitor to watch over the progress of the state's compliance. The court-appointed monitor would later create a technical assistance panel to aid in enforcing the benchmarks set. Another layer of oversight was a court-appointed special master. And, to arbitrate any problems that might arise between the parents of disabled children and the schools, the court appointed a special panel. The state would bear all the costs of compliance and pay for the plaintiffs' legal fees as well.

If this were a made-for-television movie, the closing act would portray Jennifer Felix receiving all the services she needs and would depict her mother and perhaps the attorneys as the champions of justice on behalf of all disabled children. But the next acts of this particular drama were more like the final chapters of *A Civil Action*, Jonathan Harr's harrowing account of one lawyer's failed battle against corporate malfeasance, in which justice is replaced by frustration and failure.

Jennifer Felix remained in a residential facility in Texas after the lawsuit was filed. The suit resulted in a consent decree by which the state agreed to pay for special education services for Jennifer and the other children in the Felix class. Hawaii paid $5,000 per month for Jennifer's care and also provided funds for her mother to fly to Texas and to fly Jennifer home twice each year. Franki-Servetti-Coleman reported that she was doing well there, but in a cruel irony, when the case was settled in 1994, the state of Hawaii became the decision-maker for Jennifer and the other special education children in the Felix class.

In 1998, when Jennifer was twenty-five years old, the state agencies in charge of Felix compliance decided that she was ready to move back to a program in Hawaii. When her parents objected, the case was reviewed by a panel consisting of three "experts" in the field of disability and mental health. The panel, whose existence was a product of the now-named Felix consent decree, ruled that Jennifer should be moved back to a program at Kula Hospital.

Kula Hospital, located on Maui, began operations in 1909 as a tuberculosis facility. In 1936 the Kula Sanitarium, with two hundred beds for TB patients, became an addition to the hospital. By the 1960s, Kula began offering psychiatric care, and during the 1970s it evolved into a long-term care facility. In fiscal year 1999, there were thirty-six admissions and 37,934 patient days.[3] Patient services included:

- Limited Acute Care
- Inpatient Skilled Nursing and Intermediate Care
- Developmentally Disabled Inpatient Services (ICF-MR)
- Alzheimer's and Dementia Care
- Family Practice Clinic Services
- Pharmacy
- Physical and Occupational Therapy
- Laboratory and X-ray Services
- Outpatient Clinic

Even a cursory reading of the hospital's website suggests that this was probably not the best choice for Jennifer. Her parents were totally against the move. But the state was in charge now, and the move was made. According to her mother, Jennifer's behavior totally deteriorated at Kula. She did not fit in with the kids in the program. Frankie Servetti-Coleman pointed out that even the admitting physician had asked, "What is she doing here?"

A month after coming back from Texas, Jennifer fell and shattered her knee, and spent three months at Maui Memorial Hospital. From there she was moved to Hale Lokahi, a group home facility operated by the Developmental Disabilities Services Branch of the State Department of Health. Even at Hale Lokahi, the programs and services did not meet Jennifer's needs. So her mother took action again, flying in the director of the Sequin Community Living Program in Texas, where Jennifer had lived, to come to Maui and work with the Hale Lokahi staff on a structured program for Jennifer.

In 2000, Jennifer was living in Hale Lokahi. During the day she worked at the Kokua Mau Work Center, assembling airline headsets by wrapping cords around the earpiece and placing them in plastic bags. She earned $120 a month. In May 2000, Jennifer was pictured in the *Honolulu Star* after winning a swimming race in the Hawaii Special Olympics.

Today, in 2011, Jennifer, thirty-eight, lives in Maui, in a home owned by her parents. Three full-time aides live with her in the home. Notwithstanding some severe problems—which include running away and sustaining injuries for repeatedly beating her head against the floor—Jennifer's mother reports that Jennifer has been stable for the last two years.

In the end, and with great difficulty, Frankie Servetti-Coleman got something of a storybook outcome: "Servetti-Coleman told the *Honolulu Star Advertiser* that she feels very fortunate her daughter is so much better and appears to be happy and 'goes to the pool every day. She has yoga on Thursday, out to lunch on Fridays.'"[4]

Jennifer improved mostly because she was fortunate to have an assertive family, and due to, or perhaps in spite of, the government's efforts brought about by the lawsuit. By the time Jennifer found a home in Hale Lokahi, she had aged out of the Felix class and Medicaid paid the costs of her care.

INSIDE THE EFFORTS TO MEET THE NEEDS OF DISABLED SCHOOLCHILDREN

To be fair, circumstances did improve for emotionally disturbed and special-needs children in Hawaii as a result of the class action suit and settlement. In June 2005, after twelve years of litigation and court oversight, the federal court finally dismissed the suit. In that fiscal year, the state was spending $306 million for special education services. The court left the state departments of education and health to sustain a system of care that met the needs of special education and emotionally disturbed schoolchildren. By 2010 there were nineteen thousand children designated as "special education" in the Hawaii school system. Nearly eight thousand state employees worked with special education children, and one-fifth of Hawaii's education budget—$542 million—was devoted to special education.[5] But the path to improvement was bumpy, and parents and advocates argue that special education continues to fall short of meeting the children's full needs.[6]

A Closer Look at the Felix Settlement

Between 1999 and 2001, I had the opportunity to review more than fifty case files of children in the Felix class. I found that, prior to the lawsuit, there were few services available. It took some time for the education and health departments to recruit trained personnel and put programs and systems into place. By 2000 the state had made a good start. But the start was not good enough for Judge Ezra, who found the state in contempt. The contempt decree put more pressure on the state, which responded with more funding and more focused activity.

A number of parents I spoke with were grateful for the services their children received and felt that the Felix suit was a great success. On the other hand, many parents, school personnel, and government officials were extremely frustrated at the way the state went about trying to meet the demands of the consent decree and achieve compliance with the provisions of IDEA.

Bumps in the Road

Despite some success stories and a general upgrading in services and programs, the good feelings about compliance were shared primarily among the principal players in the executive branch—the attorney general's office, the Department of Health, the court-appointed monitor, and perhaps the governor's office. Five years after the case was closed, parents and school personnel continued to be frustrated and often outraged by their inability to access the system of care. The legislature, bullied by the lawsuit into complying with every funding request, became increasingly alarmed when the cost of compliance topped 1 billion dollars, and the compliance deadline came and went without judicial approval. To make matters worse, the Felix case went into a downward spiral of scandal and corruption in 2001.

In June 2001, the legislature appointed a special committee to investigate the Felix compliance efforts. The committee took an aggressive posture and subpoenaed witnesses, including the court-appointed monitor and his staff. Judge Ezra quickly quashed the subpoenas and warned the legislature about the separation of powers between the legislative branch and the federal judicial branch. The hearings went on without the monitor and his staff, and the witnesses who did testify began to raise questions about funding patterns.

First, they questioned the fact that the head of the Health Department's Community and Adolescent Mental Health Division had hired her husband to run a newly initiated program for Felix-class children. He quickly resigned his position. Next, the special legislative committee heard testimony that questioned a $600,000 contract given by the Department of Education to a firm on the Big Island of Hawaii. An official of the Department of Education testified before the special committee and raised questions about the firm's qualifications in the field of special education and the $170,000 salary of the project's coordinator—whose prior experience included little education or special education work. A Department of Education witness and the media pointed out that the project coordinator had been a hula dancer.

Basically, the DOE witness charged that the contract was fixed and that the agency was not qualified to receive such an award. The superintendent of schools, Paul LeMahieu, first denied that he had "fixed" the contract. A month later, he admitted that he had a brief affair with the coordinator/former hula dancer. He then tendered his resignation to the Board of Education, which quickly accepted it. The final scene of this act was LeMahieu's surprise that his resignation was indeed accepted, whereupon he made an unsuccessful attempt to withdraw his resignation offer.

Two months after the superintendent's resignation, another player in the Felix case had a day in court. Leonore Behar was the former head of the child and family services section of North Carolina's state mental health division. Behar had been hired by the Felix court-appointed monitor to provide technical assistance to the Hawaii Department of Health in the compliance efforts with the settlement agreement. Behar had also provided independent consulting in Hawaii on mental health services and was the coauthor of a proposal submitted to the state for program funding. In December 2001, Behar pleaded guilty in federal court to the charge of obstructing justice. The case stemmed from Behar's efforts to prevent federal investigators from obtaining records documenting $18,000 she had funneled to herself as a consulting fee. Behar's guilty plea was part of a plea agreement in which she agreed to pay $274,000 in restitution, and in return forty-five other charges, including embezzlement, wire fraud, and stealing federal money, would be dropped.

In spring 2002, another case of fiscal mismanagement surfaced, albeit on a much smaller level. Susan Puapuaga, who worked with Alakai Na Keiki, which provided services for special-needs children on Oahu, was accused of submitting claims for $1,800 for services she did not provide. She pleaded no contest to ten counts of medical assistance fraud.

MY OWN FINDINGS

My involvement with the Felix case was serendipitous. My colleague and then dean of the School of Social Work at the University of Pennsylvania, Ira Schwartz, had consulted for the state of Hawaii on issues related to juvenile delinquents held in institutional settings. Ira had established good working relationships with state officials and influential state legislators. By December 1999, state legislators were concerned about the rising costs of the Felix settlement. The legislative auditor, Marion Higa, was worried about the lack of accountability and control over the funds that were being spent. Ms. Higa's office had already analyzed the efforts to comply with the Felix consent decree. She wanted to repeat the analysis, but this time she wanted someone from off the Islands to evaluate the compliance efforts. Ira called and asked me to draft a proposal, and by January we had been contracted to examine the situation of disabled children and IDEA compliance.

Ira and I reviewed numerous documents and traveled to Hawaii to interview state officials, state legislators, educators, and parents. As mentioned earlier, we also were able to review fifty case files of children included in the Felix class—that is, children who were eligible for services under the provision of IDEA, and to whom the state of Hawaii was required to provide services based on the consent decree.

In our initial report, we acknowledged the endeavor of all involved in the compliance efforts. Our opening statement was:

> One thing is quite clear: the Department of Health, Department of Education, Office of the Attorney General, Family Court, and the State Legislature have engaged in an immense amount of work to comply with the conditions of the *Felix* decree. From a point where the *Felix* class numbered less than 2,000 children, until the present when the class is in excess of 10,000, the departments and the legislature have expended enormous effort to not only comply with the stipulations of the consent decree, but also to provide needed services to the school children in Hawaii who have special education and/or mental health needs. The legislature should be commended for their willingness to commit funds to the

compliance effort. We attended a meeting of the House of Representatives Finance Committee held February 14, 2000, and were impressed with how cooperative and supportive the legislature is with a request for emergency and supplemental funds for Department of Health's efforts for the *Felix* class.

There is no question that department administrators, staff, and the legislature are all in agreement with the need for compliance by June 30, 2000.

Our initial impression is that nearly all the students in Hawaii who are deemed eligible for services under IDEA and/or Section 504 are receiving services or will soon receive services. No one we met with disputes the need to comply with the decree and meet students' educational and mental health needs. If a student is identified as a member of the *Felix* class and if services are available, the services are provided. If the services are not available, efforts are underway to provide those services.

Clearly, compliance and achievement of the benchmarks are goals agreed upon by all the stakeholders we met with.

In truth, that statement was an attempt to calm the waters before we began to roil them by moving on to our more critical findings:

The compliance effort has produced the unintended consequence of creating an open-ended entitlement for special education children and children with mental health issues and problems. The size of the *Felix* class has expanded dramatically, as have expenditures, which even with the imperfect accounting of *Felix* class costs have approached $250 million. Clearly, the Department of Health and the Department of Education are providing more and more services. However, there appears to be no attempt to assure that such services are effective, cost-effective, and the least intrusive.

Department administrators have a clear grasp of the exact definition of IDEA and Section 504 (i.e. *Felix* class) children. We accept without question the statement that both departments have provided training such that line staff are knowledgeable about the legal definition of IDEA and Section 504 students. What we are not assured of is that a consistent *working definition* of the *Felix* class exists across departments, school complexes, mental health agencies and professionals, service providers, parents, and other stakeholders. Although the officials at the Department of Health report they have been in contact with children's mental health officials in other states, we are not convinced that they have selected the appropriate comparison states, nor have they devoted sufficient attention and concern with identifying, developing, and implementing an appropriate and reliable working definition of the *Felix* class. This situation creates a number of important potential problems, including:

- No ability to predict how large the *Felix* class will be
- No ability to assure that the "best practices" working definition is being used
- No ability to assure that diagnoses are reliably conducted by IEP teams and/or contracted mental health professionals

A second factor that has unintentionally created the apparent open-ended entitlement is the lack of effort or even concern with assessing, using appropriate scientific methods, the effectiveness and cost-effectiveness of services provided to the children in the *Felix* class. It is extremely troubling that the Director and Deputy Director of the Department of Health believe that the terms of the consent decree and the benchmarks *do not* include a mandate to provide effective services to children. Equally troubling is the Deputy Attorney General's overt dismissal of the direct or even implied mandate that the Department of Health and Department of Education provide *effective services* to the children in the *Felix* class.

We found that the system of care created in response to the *Felix* consent decree has not achieved the expected results. The system of care focused more on procedural compliance rather than on a system to effectively help the children. In addition, the system is largely based on treatments that cannot demonstrate effectiveness. As a result, a major shift in school-based delivery of services was necessary. This involved the assumption of responsibility for mental health care for approximately six thousand children by the Department of Education.

I was most upset about the conclusion that all the effort and money spent to comply with the consent decree had seemingly failed to improve the education and lives of the six thousand or more children who made up the Felix class in 2001.

Our conclusions were not popular, and that is an understatement. One afternoon the legislative auditor's staff had literally to sneak Ira and me into the state house for a meeting with the Speaker of the House. Just our presence there was enough to set off alarms and recriminations about our report. I was not upset about being the messenger who was targeted to be shot; I was upset about the false promise that the entire Felix case produced. It was later that day that I was reminded of the third lie and government's inability to be helpful.

The government of Hawaii's efforts to help children such as Jennifer Felix fell short of the mark in many ways. The state bureaucracy consistently engaged in actions that frustrated and angered parents. One parent of an autistic daughter reported that he diligently searched the Web for information about autism. He discovered a site devoted to promising new treatment approaches. When he tried to get the Department of Education to examine the recommended services, he was turned away. It is of some note, too, that this was no ordinary parent; he was a legislative aid to a member of the Hawaii House of Representatives.

By 2001, the Department of Health finally did come around and began to provide services to autistic children—services that appeared to be helpful. But in July 2002, the department proposed to transfer these services to the public schools, a move that would affect 550 autistic children. The parents immediately raised questions about the level of care their children would receive and what impact changing caregivers would have. Given that many autistic children prefer particular structures, routines, and schedules, a change in caregivers could have a serious negative impact.

The agency directors and staff argued for the transfer, and the parents objected, pointing to the fact that, with the transfer, the Department of Education's budget for services for autistic children would receive one-half of the funding that had been budgeted by the Department of Health. After parents testified before the legislative committee examining the Felix compliance efforts, the transfer was put on hold for another year, meaning the parents would have to wage another fight twelve months later.

THE FAILURE OF GOOD INTENTIONS

One rule that I try to follow in my research and teaching is, "Data is not the plural of anecdote." I am cautious in drawing conclusions from one state's bungled efforts to comply with a federal law. On the other hand, much of what I saw in Hawaii was infuriatingly similar to what I see in other instances of the government's involvement in residual, targeted, or means-tested social policy.

The core problem with residual polices is that they require gatekeeping to determine eligibility or need. In fact, the debate to determine who is eligible is really a debate about who is "worthy" and who is "not worthy" of government assistance. Arguing to keep the gate opening as narrow as possible are those who prefer small government as well as those skeptical or simply opposed to what they refer to as "another big government program." Those who lobby for a wider opening would really prefer a universal program but are willing to settle for a residual program with somewhat permeable boundaries. In the end, some form of compromise is reached.

When the policy is implemented, it is typically under the aegis of those who wish to provide the most extensive help as possible. I have been involved in the education of nearly two thousand social workers and I have worked with thousands more. I can say with reasonable conviction that students and professionals believe that social justice will be best served if the access gates to social programs are opened as wide as possible.

This is a value position that they apply to all their work. But there is also a pragmatic reason for keeping the gates open. The perverse incentive of residual social policies is that the wider the opening, the more funding there is for personnel and services. In Hawaii, a larger population of students labeled "eligible for special education" expanded the career opportunities for teachers, psychologists, and other service providers (including former hula dancers). The educators and human service providers knew the state budget was tight and that there would be little chance of funding increases for basic education or mental health services. But the Felix consent decree was a loophole, a means to "backdoor" funding for education and services.

The bigger the eligible population, the more the state will have to fund, or else be found in contempt of the consent decree. In child welfare, Title IV-E funding flows to states, localities, and private agencies that provide foster care for children. Title IV-E funding pays for food and clothing for each child, and for each child in care there is also funding for training or administrative costs. Thus, while foster care is supposed to be short-term, the longer a child stays in care, the more administrative and training funding the providing agency receives. Clearly, there is a perverse incentive to prolong stays in foster care.

The efforts to prop open the gates or even weld them open permanently produce two important consequences. First, there is likely to be a need to employ more gatekeepers to keep up with the demand for reviewing eligibility. Thus, the front end of a residual program often has a costly and elaborate infrastructure (or bureaucracy)— e.g., child protective service investigators, as well as the psychologists in Hawaii who led the Individual Education Program teams. Second, because funding is not really inexhaustible, the more open the gate, the more diluted the services available for those deemed to be in need or eligible.

Equally troubling is the fact that once the services are provided, there may be an incentive for clients not to improve. I do not want to overstate this accusation, but the fact is that in some residual programs too few people actually get better. In our review of the children in the Felix class in Hawaii, we noted that in almost every case services increased, but there was no notation or finding that the child was "improving" or could actually "step down" in services. In the foster care system, nearly twenty thousand children each year "age out" of the system—that is, they reach the age of majority and are no longer eligible for services. But the fact that they do not receive services from the child welfare system does not mean they are ready to take on the role of healthy and productive adults.

It is the residual nature of so many social programs that makes them ineffective. The gamesmanship of gatekeeping, the diluted services, and the often self-serving and self-protecting bureaucracy conspire to make something of a joke out of so many government efforts. Conservatives may rejoice in my lambasting government social programs, and liberals may write off my critique as merely anecdotal (if an entire state's failed program can be considered an anecdote). But the takeaway is that residual social programs that depend on gatekeeping to deliver help are fundamentally flawed.

Chapter 3

PROGRAMS THAT WORK

One of the best pieces of news to come out of my research is that there are in fact government programs that actually help those for whom they are intended. Both statistical and anecdotal evidence support this conclusion. The programs are cost-effective and require a relatively small federal bureaucracy. And they have positive ripple effects beyond their original intent. What are these programs and what makes them superior to others?

Throughout the gestation period of this book, I have quizzed friends, colleagues, policymakers, and the occasional passerby about which government programs they believe are actually effective. My query typically produces a halt in the conversation, a quizzical look, and some head scratching—after which a few candidates may be offered, sometimes correctly, sometimes incorrectly. Among my academic colleagues, the most frequent guess is "Head Start."

HEAD START

Head Start is a classic residual means-tested program. A component of Lyndon Johnson's War on Poverty, it was part of the Economic Opportunity Act of 1964.[1] The purpose of the Act itself was to "mobilize the human and financial resources of the Nation to combat poverty in the United States." Head Start was designed to meet the educational and nutritional needs of disadvantaged preschool children. It began in 1965 as an eight-week summer program.

A little more than forty years later, Head Start has an annual federal appropriation of nearly $8 billion and serves approximately 900,000 children, most of whom are under four years of age. Head Start is more than simply early education for disadvantaged children. It also provides social and health care services, with the goal of ensuring that poor children are prepared and ready to start school. The federal means test for enrollment is that the family must be at 100 percent of the federal poverty level. Local programs can also establish entry criteria, including disabilities. Up to 10 percent of the children enrolled can come from families above the federal poverty line.[2] Head Start is relatively inexpensive on a per-pupil basis, about $7,000 per child, and the workforce is modest, with nearly 250,000 paid employees and a substantial number of volunteers.

Is the conventional wisdom correct that Head Start is a government program that "works"? Well, it kind of depends on what one means by "works." A three-year study of the program's effectiveness, funded by the federal government and begun in 1992, compared traditional classroom-based Head Start to family home daycare settings. The study concluded that:[3]

- Family child care homes (a form of daycare) were able to meet the requirements of the Head Start Program Performance Measures and appear to be a viable option for delivery of Head Start services.
- By the end of the program year, children assigned to family child care homes performed at least as well as those in Head Start center classrooms on measures of school readiness.
- Parent outcomes did not differ significantly by setting.
- Children in the two settings performed equally well in kindergarten on measures of cognitive, social-emotional, and physical outcomes.
- Program quality measures were correlated with children's scores on cognitive development, both in the program year and in the kindergarten follow-up year.

The economist Steven Levitt and writer Stephen Dubner take a deeper look at Head Start's achievements, beyond parental involvement and school readiness. In their best-selling book, *Freakonomics*,[4] they conclude that Head Start has no lasting effects on children. In their study, whatever gains the children served by Head Start achieved over comparable children who were not in Head Start had disappeared by the time the children reached fourth grade.

A more nuanced conclusion is offered by social and public policy scholars Katherine Magnuson, Christopher Ruhm, and Jane Waldfogel.[5] Their analysis of pre-kindergarten programs similar to Head Start found that they improve reading and mathematics skills at school entry, but they also increase behavioral problems and reduce children's self-control. Furthermore, the effects of pre-kindergarten programs on skills largely dissipate by the spring of first grade, although the behavioral effects do not. Finally, effects were found to differ depending on family background and subsequent schooling: disadvantaged children and those attending schools with low levels of academic instruction showed the largest and most lasting academic gains. Finally, the most recent and comprehensive federal examination of Head Start found small gains for the three-year-olds and few gains for the four-year-olds.[6]

This book is not the place to engage deeply in an examination of the effectiveness of Head Start. As with nearly all outcome evaluations of government programs, the results often depend on the methodology, measures, and time frame. Nonetheless, it appears that the long-term impact of an inexpensive federal program that enrolls fewer than one million children per year is, at best, modest.

The Earned Income Tax Credit (EITC)

Among my colleagues who specialize in public policy and programs aimed at the poor, the answer to "What works?" often includes the "Earned Income Tax Credit" (EITC). EITC is indeed a significant exception to the third-lie joke about government.[7]

In brief, EITC is a refundable tax credit for people who earn less than 200 percent of the federal poverty level each year. EITC is administered and operated through the federal income tax code. The EITC continues to receive bipartisan support because it encourages work while at the same time providing income support to low-income families. The means testing to determine eligibility is done through the Internal Revenue Code and taxation system, and the same system that manages tax payments and refunds also provides the payments under the EITC. Unlike tax refunds, which come in one check (or may be applied toward future tax liabilities), EITC payments may be paid out over time as part of weekly or monthly wages (although this option does not seem to be used by many recipients[8]).

The EITC payment is based on the family size and annual earnings of the taxpayer. In 2010, a family with three children could earn a tax credit of up to $5,666; families with two children would earn up to $5,036; families with one child earn a maximum of $3,050; and families without children earn $457.[9]

EITC is the largest federal cash assistance program in existence today, although this is not widely known outside of policy circles. In 2008, 24 million taxpayers received $49 billion in reduced taxes and refunds. According to the Center for Budget and Policy Priorities, EITC lifted 6.6 million people, including 3.3 million children, out of poverty in 2009.[10] The few criticisms leveled at EITC focus on its escalating costs (it is adjusted for inflation each year, unlike most other federal targeted programs), the complicatedness of the application process, and the high margin of error—the error rate in IRS forms is the highest among all federal antipoverty programs.[11] Of course, with inflation minimal in 2009–2010, EITC adjustments have also been minimal.[12] On the other hand, the complexity of the application process means that tax preparers may be gaining a portion of the federal benefits provided by EITC. EITC's cost-effective management provides some guidance for programs that could work. Liberal think tanks, such as the Center for Budget and Policy Priorities, consider EITC a highly effective federal program, and its success has motivated many states to enact their own versions.[13] Conservative think tanks also support EITC because of its cost-effectiveness.[14]

WELFARE REFORM

In his 1993 State of the Union address, President Bill Clinton promised to "end welfare as we know it." Welfare, as we knew it in 1993, was a residue of the Social Security Act of 1935. A component of the Social Security Act of 1935, Aid to Dependent Children (ADC), had become Aid to Families with Dependent Children (AFDC). A program to assist children of low-income families became a program that provided funding directly to parents who had little or no income. In the 1930s the parents were often widows and the children were often orphans. By the 1990s, the parents were largely single mothers whose children had two parents who were not married to each other.

AFDC was an "open-ended entitlement," which means that the federal funding was not capped and that the federal government would match state funding for parents with little or no income. By 1996, AFDC was spending $24 billion per year. Time limits for receipts of benefits were a bit flexible, or lax, depending on your point of view, and the benefit allocation increased if a recipient had another child. AFDC was the perfect target for reform. The benefits were insufficient to raise mothers and their children above poverty, and there were no incentives for recipients to enter the workforce, since working might cause them to lose what benefits they were receiving.

Bill Clinton was unable to end welfare as we knew it after his 1993 State of the Union address, but the Congressional election of 1994 brought in a Republican majority in both the House of Representatives and the Senate. Representative Newt Gingrich organized a campaign strategy entitled "The Contract with America." When Gingrich became Speaker of the House in January, 1995, one core component of the "contract" was welfare reform. The first two versions of the Republican welfare reform plan—the Personal Responsibility Act—were vetoed by President Clinton.[15] But the third iteration, the Personal Responsibility and Work Opportunity Act of 1996 (Pub.L. 104-193), was signed by the President on August 26, 1996.

If one were to judge the effectiveness of welfare reform, or the Personal Responsibility and Work Opportunity Act of 1996, by whether or not it reduced poverty, we would have a powerful example of the third lie. But the fact is that PRWORA, as the act ended up being called, was never intended to decrease poverty. The reformers' goals were to incentivize work and provide disincentives for remaining on welfare. The open-ended entitlement of AFDC was abolished and replaced with capped block grants to the states. The new law provided stipulations that the states must meet to qualify for the block grants. These were mainly time limits for receiving benefits (sixty months) and work requirements—a specific percentage of welfare recipients were required to enter the workforce if they received welfare benefits for two consecutive years. Indirectly, the legislation attempted to encourage marriage and discourage out-of-marriage birth. If some legislators had had their way, the bill would not have increased payments with the birth of another child, but this was not included in the final legislation.

The rate of poverty in the United States was about 15 percent in 1993 and had declined to 14 percent by the time PRWORA was passed. The rate went as low as 12 percent prior to the 2001 recession and was up to 14.3 percent in 2009.

For children under eighteen, the poverty rate stood at 22 per thousand in 1993, was at about 19.8 per thousand when PRWORA passed, declined to a low of 15.6 per thousand prior to the 2001 recession, and was back up to 20.1 per thousand in 2009. PRWORA had no major lasting impact on raising children above the poverty level, but then again that was not the purpose of the legislation.

The immediate impact of PRWORA was a decrease in the number of recipients of welfare benefits (called Temporary Assistance to Needy Families, or TANF).[16] According to the Census Bureau, between 1996 and 2000 there was a 50 percent decrease in the number of mothers receiving TANF payments. There were 12.6 million recipients of AFDC benefits in 1996. This number dropped to less than 6 million in 2000 and under 4 million in 2002—after a national recession. The number of children receiving benefits declined from 12.5 million in 1996 to 5.3 million in 2002.[17] In 2006, two years

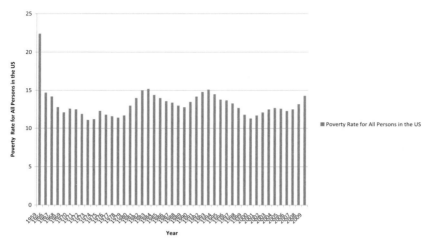

Figure 3. Poverty Rate in the United States 1959–2009.

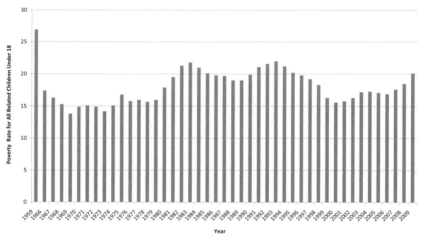

Figure 4. Poverty Rate for Related Children under Age 18.

before the economic events that led to the 2008 recession, an average of 4.14 million individuals received welfare benefits, or which 3.1 million were children.[18] At the onset of the recession, the number of welfare recipients declined to 3.7 million and the number of children was down to 2.9 million.[19] In 2010, the Administration on Children and Families reported that the number of welfare recipients had risen to 4.3 million and the number of children was up to 3.2 million.[20] Clearly, the economic downturn had a significant effect on low-income mothers and their children.

The House of Representatives Committee on Ways and Means also notes that the average size of a family receiving TANF benefits dropped from 3.9 persons in 1970 to 2.5 persons in 2002.[21] Of course, the size of all households in the United States declined in that quarter-century, so the true test of PRWORA is whether out-of-marriage births among poor women declined. Overall, and for each racial or ethnic group, the rate of out-of-marriage births increased from 1996 to 2005.[22] However, the out-of-marriage birthrate for women sixteen to nineteen years of age declined from 1996 until 2005, when it went up.[23] The decline cut across all racial and ethnic groups, as did the 2005 increase. There are too many factors related to out-of-marriage births to draw any meaningful conclusion as to whether welfare reform had any influence at all on out-of-marriage births among poor women. This same multitude of factors made it equally difficult to make this determination prior to welfare reform.

If we judge welfare reform by the criteria and metrics embraced by the legislators and advocates who fought for it, the change from an open-ended entitlement to block grants and the establishment of work requirements and time limits generated the desired results. The main result—a decrease in caseloads—persisted through the 2001 recession and continued until 2008. Even in the aftermath of the 2008 recession, the number of welfare recipients has not climbed up to the 1996 figures (12.6 million recipients and 8.6 million children).[24] It is clear that the outcome of welfare reform was not just the result of a strong economy in the 1990s. One policy dilemma that remains unanswered is why some 3 million individuals eligible for TANF were not choosing to participate in 2010.

SEVENTY YEARS OF SUCCESS: THE SOCIAL SECURITY ACT OF 1935

When I pose the question "Which government program has been the most successful?" it does not take long for someone to name the Social Security Act of 1935. The success of the act, some seventy years later, is seen in the fact that we have come to take its benefits for granted.

Born out of the Great Depression and enacted late in President Franklin D. Roosevelt's first term, the Social Security Act was signed into law on August 15, 1935. The early part of Roosevelt's New Deal focused on social welfare programs that provided relief in the form of jobs, bonuses for veterans, and public relief. Two years before the enactment of the Social Security Act, Congress established the Federal Emergency Relief Administration (FERA), which directed $500 million to state and local welfare agencies. Half of the FERA funds ($250 million) were dedicated to match state expenditures with federal government spending, providing $1 for each $3 of state and local spending. The other $250 million were distributed based on need and did not require a match.

Relief was primarily aimed at creating work for those in need. But cash payments were given to heads of families who were employable, but still could not find work. Although FERA was followed by the enactment of the Works Progress Administration (WPA), which ultimately funded jobs for 8 million Americans,[25] many employable heads of families continued to receive direct relief in the form of cash payments.

The Social Security Act of 1935 marked a dramatic change in government approaches to social welfare. Numerous forces combined to move Congress and the Roosevelt administration away from its reluctance to provide old-age and unemployment insurance. But by 1935, the coalescence of the Depression and the increase in the number of people sixty-five or older forced Congress' hand.

Several books and articles examine the history of the Social Security Act of 1935.[26] While the general public may not be aware of the details of the act itself, what that act is and does is clear from its own description. Public Law 271 was enacted to:

> provide for the general welfare by establishing a system of Federal old-age benefits, and by establishing the several States to make for adequate provision for aged person, blind persons, dependent and crippled children, maternal and child welfare, public health, and the administration of their unemployment compensation laws; to establish a Social Security Board; to raise revenue; and for other purposes.[27]

Title II of the Act established old-age benefits by creating an account in the Treasury of the United States to be known as the "Old-Age Reserve Account." Monies would be deposited into the account sufficient to pay the premiums required under the act (I will discuss the reserve account later).

A qualified person would receive payments when he (no "she" appeared in the act) reached the qualifying age of sixty-five. Qualifications were based on eligibility criteria described in Section 210 of the act. The recipient had to be at least sixty-five and have collected not less than $2,000 in total wages after December 31, 1936 and before turning sixty-five. Title II also provided payments to the estate of qualified persons who died before turning sixty-five. Those who were not qualified under Section 210 would receive a lump sum payment upon reaching sixty-five.

The Social Security reserve account was appropriated $4 million for the fiscal year ending June 30, 1936, and a sum of $49 million for each fiscal year thereafter. The reserve account was initially financed by a tax on wages, in which employers and employees would each pay a 1 percent tax (or "contribution," depending on one's point of view) on base wages up to a maximum taxable amount of $3,000 per year. Thus, a worker would pay a maximum of $30 per year in Social Security taxes and this would be matched by the employer. At sixty-five a single worker would receive $22 per month, and a married worker would receive $36. In order for the reserve fund to accumulate reserves, no payments were made to eligible workers until 1940.

Title II of the Social Security Act has been revised over the last seventy years, with increases in the tax rate, the maximum amount taxed, the eligibility age, and the amount of the monthly benefit. Thus, by 2009, the tax rate for employees and employers was 7.65 percent and the tax was applicable for wages up to $106,800.[28] In 2009, the maximum Social Security tax paid by an individual (and matched by the employer) was $8,170. Full retirement age has also increased, so that people born in 1943 can receive full benefits at age sixty-six. Ultimately, the full retirement age will be sixty-seven for anyone born after 1960. Benefits, if one was sixty-five in 2009 and worked enough to be eligible for full benefits, will be $27,876 per year. There is no reduction in benefits for someone who earns additional wages at full retirement age.

Other titles in the Social Security Act are mostly targeted or means-tested programs for specific categories—such as the blind, disabled, and children placed in out-of-home care. The latter programs, including Temporary Assistance for Needy Family (TANF), which grew out of Aid to Families with Dependent Children (AFDC), which grew out of Title IV of the Social Security Act (ADC), are not considered widely successful. These means-tested government programs have been at the core of debates about who is worthy and unworthy. In addition, these categorical programs require substantial bureaucracies to apply the worthy/unworthy eligibility tests.

The Impact of Social Security Benefits

What were referred to as the "old-age" benefits of the Social Security Act (Title II) did not have an immediate impact. As mentioned, the government delayed paying benefits until 1940 so that the reserve account would have adequate assets to make payments. The percentage of eligible recipients was less than 50 percent until 1960. The percent of the elderly receiving Social Security benefits reached nearly 90 percent in 1975 and has remained at that level into the twenty-first century. In 2010, nearly 37.4 million people were receiving old-age and survivors insurance.[29]

Old-age and survivor benefits gradually removed much of the burden for the care of the elderly from the children of aging parents. It is difficult to measure the emotional, social, and economic impact this change produced, but it is obvious that monies and energies that would have been devoted to the care of aging parents were spent in other ways. A more measurable impact is the percentage of the elderly who live in poverty. In 1959, just prior to the time when more than half of those over sixty-five were receiving Social Security benefits, 35.9 percent of those elderly lived in poverty. By 2009, the percentage of seniors living in poverty had declined to 8.9 percent. On the other hand, the poverty rate for those eighteen to sixty-four years of age was 17 percent in 1959 and 12.9 percent in 2009. The poverty rate for children under eighteen was 27 percent in 1959 and 20.1 percent in 2009.[30] Poverty among the elderly declined 75 percent, while among children the decline was 23 percent, and for everyone else the decline was 24 percent.

Social Security Is Going Broke and Other Issues

Numerous criticisms have been aimed at the old-age benefits of the Social Security Act. The tax is too high, the benefits are too low, the cost-of-living increases are too high or too low, and so on. One early criticism was that the promise of old-age benefits would depress private savings. And, in fact, over the years Americans have saved less. From 1960 to 1979 private savings made up 11 percent of the national income. By 2005, this figure had declined to 3.9 percent.[31] Social Security benefits may partially explain this decline, but many other factors account for the precipitous drop in personal savings in the United States.

The main criticism of Social Security is that "it is going broke." There are many ways of expressing this argument. Starting in 1975 and continuing to 1981, the Old-Age and Survivors Insurance Fund suffered a net decrease in funds and a deficit in the Social Security reserve account from $890 million to as high as $4.9 billion.[32] Projecting out the rate of decline, the reserve account would have been depleted by 1983. Congress initially addressed this problem by enacting the Social Security Amendments of 1983 (Public Law 98-21), which modified the manner in which cost-of-living adjustments (COLA's) were calculated. The law also imposed a tax on benefits that exceeded $25,000 for an individual and $32,000 for a couple. Finally, the age at which people could receive full benefits was gradually increased.

Other arguments related to the predicted insolvency of old-age and survivor benefits include:

- Changes in the number of workers it would take to support a recipient of benefits. The Heritage Foundation estimated that in 1950 sixteen workers supported each recipient; in 1997 the ratio was down to three to one, and by 2030 the ratio is forecasted to be two to one.[33]
- Americans are living longer and recipients will receive benefits for a longer period of time.
- At some point, demographic factors, the strength (or weakness) of the economy, and the benefit rate will exhaust the reserve account and the payout of benefits will be far greater than the tax revenue received from workers and employers. What year this will occur depends on the economy as well as the tax rate and the upper threshold for Social Security taxes.

The Social Security reserve account, or what is often called the Trust Fund, deserves special mention. For a long time I was under the assumption, along with many others, that my Social Security taxes, along with taxes paid by my employer, were being deposited in a reserve account. Once I reached retirement age I would receive payments from *my* account. My assumption is reinforced once a year when the Social Security Administration sends me a report that details my entire work history, my total wages, my Social Security wages, and the amount of tax I have paid (doubling that amount to include my employer's contribution yields the total tax paid).

It turns out, of course, that I have no such "account." Each year the government takes in Social Security taxes and pays out Social Security benefits. Any surplus is used to fund other government programs. Writing for the Heritage Foundation, Daniel Mitchell stated that the Trust Fund is a *hoax*: it "contains nothing more than IOUs—money the government owes itself. The annual surpluses that many thought were being used to build up a reserve for baby boomers have been spent on other government programs, leaving the Trust Fund holding a bag of government bonds."[34]

Policymakers and pundits have debated the many options that could shore up the Social Security system. The tried and true method is to increase the tax and the income threshold. However, raising taxes is a political third rail. Raising the threshold is tempting, especially since Social Security taxes are regressive—those who make the least income pay a greater percentage than everyone above the income threshold. But raising the threshold too high, or applying it to all wages, would threaten public support of Social Security.

The wealthiest Americans already know that they won't "get out" of Social Security what they have "put in." Nonetheless, upper-income thresholds appear to be somewhat fair. Should the threshold be raised to cover all income, those at the top of the income scale will recognize that Social Security is just another government program that transfers money from the well-to-do to the "less-well-to-do." Such a policy will most certainly open the door to a debate about the "worthy" versus the "unworthy" poor, as well as an argument about "transfer of wealth." Social Security might then be viewed as a not-so-subtle residual program to help the poor.

In the 2000 presidential elections the candidates took diverse paths to dealing with Social Security. Republican candidate George Bush proposed that Social Security be privatized and that beneficiaries be able to invest their accumulated funds privately. Workers could divert some of their Social Security payroll taxes to private investment accounts, and thus generate higher rates of returns and greater benefits compared to the increases offered through Social Security cost-of-living adjustments. Democratic candidate Al Gore countered with a proposal to have government match contributions with tax credits.[35] Actually, Gore was much better known for his "lock box" proposal, which he repeated in the presidential debates: "We will balance the budget every year, and dedicate the budget surplus first to saving Social Security. Putting both Social Security and Medicare in an iron-clad lock box, where the politicians can't touch them—to me, that kind of common sense is a family value."[36]

Gore lost, and the privatization of Social Security disappeared from the policy radar screen after the events of 9/11, the dot-com collapse of 2001, and the mortgage and financial collapses of 2007 and 2008. Had people been allowed to invest some of their Social Security payroll taxes in the stock market, they most surely would have joined the millions of workers who saw large portions of their individual retirement accounts evaporate—at least for the time being.

Another suggestion is to change Social Security from an age- and work-based entitlement to a form of insurance. In other words, only those who truly "need" Social Security benefits would receive them. Simply stated, I think this would be a disaster. Changing Social Security from a universal program to a residual program would mean moving from a truly effective program to a perfect example of the third lie. First, and most important, the change would require that the law establish a means test or eligibility criterion to determine who will receive the benefits. Then a bureaucracy would have to be established to carry out the means testing. Third, there are innumerable ways individuals could "game" a means-tested system in order to qualify for Social Security benefits—for example, transferring wealth and property to spouses or children. Of course, these reasons are moot since it is just not going to happen. It is unimaginable that any legislator would propose to strip benefits from millions of individuals who have spent their working lives paying the Social Security tax and expecting to withdraw funds from "their" accounts upon retirement.

It Works

Debates over solvency notwithstanding, Social Security works as a government policy and has worked for more than seventy years. The tax structure appears fair, the benefits, while not huge, are sufficient to keep 90 percent of the elderly out of poverty, and the bureaucracy that supports Social Security never has to invest people and time to determine who should or should not receive the benefit.

THE LEGACY OF LYNDON JOHNSON'S WAR ON POVERTY: MEDICARE

By the mid-1960s the postwar economic boom had wound down and the Cold War against communism was not as heated as it had been in the Eisenhower and Kennedy administrations. Vietnam had not yet become a major issue within the United States. Poverty and disadvantage slowly began to capture public and then policy attention. Of all the writing on this topic, Michael Harrington's 1962 book, *The Other America: Poverty in the United States*,[37] received the most notice. Members of both the Kennedy and Johnson administrations paid close attention to Harrington's powerful journey through the world of the poor. His major contribution to policy was that he attributed poverty to government mismanagement and not to the personal attributes or failings of those who were poor.

President Johnson, whom future generations would link more with Vietnam than with domestic policies, crystallized his domestic policy by envisioning what he called "The Great Society." The cornerstone of the Great Society would be an attack on, and an elimination of, poverty. And so, on March 16, 1964, President Johnson sent a message to Congress declaring "a war on poverty."

Johnson's War on Poverty included a broad range of programs. Among the most enduring and best known are the Job Corps, Volunteers in Service to America (VISTA), and the Community Actions Program (CAP). But the War on Poverty, like the third lie, offered something of a false promise. As Ronald Reagan quipped, "In the sixties we fought a war on poverty, and poverty won."

The cost of Johnson's War on Poverty was high, the results unimpressive, and most of the signature programs are now gone or significantly reduced. But there was one battle in the war that can be claimed as a victory: health care for the elderly.

Public Law 89-79 was added to the Social Security Act on July 30, 1965. The name of the new program was Medicare, and its purpose was to provide the elderly with hospital insurance and the option of medical insurance.[38] Medicare has evolved into a four-part program. Part A, the compulsory Hospital Insurance, pays for inpatient hospitalization as well as some nursing home care and home health costs. Eligibility and enrollment for Part A occur on a person's sixty-fifth birthday. Part B, Supplemental Medical Insurance, is a voluntary program in which one may elect to enroll at age sixty-five. Those who enroll pay a monthly premium that helps cover doctors' services and outpatient care. It also covers, in part or totally, some other services that Part A does not cover, including physical and occupational therapy, medical supplies, and home health care.

Part C of Medicare, Medicare Advantage, is available in some parts of the country through private insurers who are approved by the Medicare program. Under this plan, those sixty-five or older may elect to receive all their health care services through a provider organization and based on the coverage offered by private insurance companies. The newest component of Medicare is Part D. Introduced in January 2006, it provides prescription drug coverage through private companies approved by Medicare. One may choose coverage under the Prescription Drug Plan (PDP) or through Medicare Advantage (if available). After a $275 deductible, recipients pay 25 percent of the cost of prescriptions. Certain drugs are excluded from coverage.

It is beyond the scope and purpose of this book to provide a full accounting of the four Medicare programs. Although some people argue that the planned coverages are not complicated, I did notice that six months before my wife would celebrate her sixty-fifth birthday we received two huge encyclopedias on Medicare—one from the federal government and a second, equally large volume from our private insurer. The federal government must have worried whether my wife had received her volume, because a few weeks later we received a duplicate Medicare encyclopedia.

Even with the detailed explanations, my wife, who holds two master's degrees, needed to seek advice from the human resources department of the University of Pennsylvania. In her case, the decision was simple (I hope). She was automatically eligible for Part A and elected not to be covered by parts B, C, and D as she was already covered by my university-based private insurance.

Medicare's strength is that it is not a means-tested program and provides, in the basic plan, a single-payer system of medical coverage for everyone sixty-five and older, along with options for other coverage. The cost of the basic insurance is financed by payroll taxes, while the supplemental plans are funded by a combination of payroll taxes and payments made by recipients. The perceived weaknesses of Medicare, however, receive considerable attention and stir up heated debate. In reality, though, the weaknesses have nothing to do with the program itself and everything to do with the problem of medical care in the United States.

Medicare is an enormous and expensive federal program that covers 45 million Americans[39] and provided $509 billion in benefits in 2009.[40] It constitutes more than one-fifth of the health care spending in the United States.[41] The core problem is rising costs, which have risen more than 10 percent per year since 1980.[42] In 1970, Medicare spending made up 1 percent of the Gross National Product (GNP) of the United States. By 1994 the proportion increased to 2.7 and by 2008 it was 3.2 percent.[43]

As with Social Security, projections forecast a depletion of Medicare trust funds and a deficit in the future. The trustees of the Social Security and Medicare trust funds now estimate that the Medicare Hospital Insurance Fund (Part A) will be exhausted by 2017.[44] Parts B and D will remain financially solvent, because the law stipulates that the revenue generated in one tax year finances the costs for the next tax year. Of course, underlying this solvency is the reality that, with a rapidly aging population, premium costs will go up to cover the rising numbers of those insured and the rising costs of health care.

If, as some say, Medicare is going broke, how can I claim it is a program that works? The answer is simple. Medicare provides single-payer health insurance for in-patient hospitalization care, funded by payroll taxes, for 22 million Americans over the age of sixty-five. The administrative expenses for Part A, health insurance, constitute a mere 1.4 percent of the total expenses.[45]

There is still the question of the overall cost of Medicare, even with the minimal administrative costs. During the first term of the Reagan administration, in 1983, Congress attempted to hold down costs by capping Medicare reimbursements for hospital stays. The concept of Diagnostically Related Groups (DRG) was introduced into Medicare billing. Under the DRG, hospitals were reimbursed based on a formula for how much a specific category of medical problem should cost to treat (as opposed to the open-ended reimbursement system). In order to maintain their cost structure, hospitals ended up discharging Medicare patients under a "quicker but sicker"[46] policy. Soon after the introduction of the DRG reimbursement system, physicians treating Medicare patients were required to accept Medicare-approved rates or else opt out of being a Medicare-approved physician.

The bottom line, that I will suggest here and leave for others to debate, is that physicians and hospitals have a perverse incentive to provide more care to Medicare patients, irrespective of whether such care is warranted or supported by scientific evidence. The "more is more" incentive is driven by the economic motivations of physicians and hospital systems, but also by the threat of malpractice litigation. The cost-fault of Medicare lies not in the government program itself, but in the larger problem of health care costs in the United States.

BUILDING MAIN STREET: THE GI BILL

The story of how the GI Bill of 1944 became law (the bill's official title was the Servicemen's Readjustment Act of 1944, P.L. 78-346) should be a simple tale of how a grateful nation welcomed back 16 million servicemen and women and rewarded them for a job well done by providing generous educational, housing, and medical benefits. Or the story could be more pragmatic, explaining how thoughtful statesmen and educators conceived of a way to productively reintroduce 16 million GI Joes and GI Janes into the economy by providing them access to education—and not just dumping them into an economy that had been focused on military production for five years.

Both narratives would play well today, but neither is accurate. Instead, the story of how the GI Bill came into being in 1944 stars a man whom one writer described as a "dyed-in-the wool racist, anti-Semitic, Red-bating, New Deal-bashing, future Dixiecrat."[47] A second chronicler of the GI Bill echoed this description by referring to the main proponent of the bill as "a brilliant legislative tactician... [and] one of the most openly bigoted racists and anti-Semites ever to serve in the House of Representatives."[48]

Representative John Rankin was probably all of these things. A Democrat, he was elected to the U.S. House of Representatives in 1920 to represent Mississippi's First District, based in Tupelo. Rankin chaired the House Committee on World War Veterans' Legislation, and was the major player in the enactment of the GI Bill.

One might have expected that enlightened educators would be the first and most vocal supporters of a legislation that would provide returning veterans an opportunity to either go back to school or take advantage of the opportunities offered by higher education. But contrary to expectations, two of the most influential university presidents opposed the GI Bill. Harvard President James Conant, commenting on an early version of the bill, predicted that it would be a disaster and would lower the quality of higher education by "failing to distinguish between those who can profit most by advanced education and those who cannot." Conant's counterpart at the University of Chicago, Robert Hutchins, predicted that the GI Bill would turn colleges into "hobo jungles" filled with veterans interested not in education, but in a monthly stipend.[49]

Even with such improbable alliances—a bigot supporting the GI Bill and the leaders of the elite educational institutions opposing it—one could still assume nostalgically that calmer and more rational voices would prevail and that Congress would overwhelmingly support the legislation. Not so. When the final version of the bill was passed by the House and the Senate, it rested with the conference committee to resolve the differences in the House and Senate versions. The conference turned out to be deadlocked three to three.

Representative John Gibson, a Democrat from Georgia, had asked Rankin to cast his proxy vote in the conference committee. Rankin refused to do this, and so on June 8, 1944, just as the Allied forces were moving off the beaches in Normandy, supporters of the GI Bill set out to find Gibson, who was hunting in Georgia. The search was literally an all-points bulletin, with radio stations telling listeners that if they knew the whereabouts of Representative Gibson they should have him call an operator in Washington. State police cars were dispatched to find Gibson, who finally answered a phone call at home.

A representative from the American Legion (supporters of the bill) got out of bed and drove Gibson to the Waycross Air Base, where a corporal and a private served as a driving team to transport him two hundred miles to Jacksonville on rain-slicked roads. From there, Gibson flew to Washington on an Eastern Airlines plane that had been held for him through the night. He landed at 6:37 a.m. and attended the 10:00 a.m. meeting of the conference committee.

Gibson's arrival and statement that he would hold a press conference and identify anyone on the committee voting against the bill swayed the committee members—Rankin included—and the vote in favor of the bill was unanimous. What we commonly call the GI Bill was approved by the Senate on June 12 and the House on June 13, 1944. Franklin Delano Roosevelt signed the bill into law on June 22, 1944.

The main components of the GI Bill were laid out in President Roosevelt's signing statement:

> This bill, which I have signed today, substantially carries out most of the recommendations made by me in a speech on July 28, 1943, and more specifically in messages to the Congress dated October 27, 1943, and November 23, 1943:
>
> 1. It gives servicemen and women the opportunity of resuming their education or technical training after discharge, or of taking a refresher or retrainer course, not only without tuition charge up to $500 per school year, but with the right to receive a monthly living allowance while pursuing their studies.
> 2. It makes provision for the guarantee by the Federal Government not to exceed 50 percent of certain loans made to veterans for the purchase or construction of homes, farms, and business properties.
> 3. It provides for reasonable unemployment allowances payable each week up to a maximum period of one year, to those veterans who are unable to find a job.
> 4. It establishes improved machinery for effective job counseling for veterans and for finding jobs for returning soldiers and sailors.
> 5. It authorizes the construction of all necessary additional hospital facilities.
> 6. It strengthens the authority of the Veterans Administration to enable it to discharge its existing and added responsibilities with promptness and efficiency.
>
> With the signing of this bill a well-rounded program of special veterans' benefits is nearly completed. It gives emphatic notice to the men and women in our armed forces that the American people do not intend to let them down.[50]

By design, the GI Bill provided veterans with education, housing, and health care benefits. The consequences were the creation of what sociologist Arlene Skolnick called a "new American middle class" and the literal, as well as figurative, construction of America's Main Street. An estimated 7.8 million World War II veterans enrolled in some sort of educational or training program.[51] Enrollment in colleges and universities increased from nearly 1.7 million in 1945, of which 5 percent (88,000) were veterans, to 2 million in 1946, of which nearly half were veterans.[52] Veteran enrollment peaked in 1947 at 65 percent, 1.5 million out of a total of 2.3 million enrollees.

Veterans enrolled in a range of colleges, universities, and training programs. They breached the Ivy League walls, probably to the chagrin of Harvard President Conant. James Wright, president of Dartmouth College, noted that in 1947, 60 percent of the incoming class at Dartmouth were veterans.[53]

The GI Bill housing benefits, in the form of the Veterans Administration loans, were not the sole policy behind the construction of Main Street, but were certainly a major catalyst. Of the 324,000 homes constructed in the United States in 1945, only 43,000 were sold on VA mortgages. The next year, housing starts jumped to slightly more than 1 million, of which 412,000 were financed by VA mortgages.[54] There were even more VA mortgage-backed new housing starts in 1947. And these numbers refer only to VA-backed new construction; many hundreds of thousands of existing homes were purchased with VA mortgages. All told, nearly 5 million veterans bought homes with GI benefits.[55]

Five million home purchases was a true "supply-side" event, in that it stimulated other economic growth. Housing developments, such as Bill Levitt's Levittowns, helped create suburbia. Building materials were needed and were created by entrepreneurial corporations. Appliances were manufactured and bought, and new appliances—including television sets—came into being. The housing boom was so robust it helped create an economy in which a single wage-earner could support a family, an economy that lasted through much of the 1950s. By then, a broad segment of the American population perceived home ownership as a goal and even a right.

The combination of education, housing purchases, and consumer economy that supported housing and suburban developments enhanced the growth of the middle class. But this was a new kind of middle class, a "gentrified" middle class.[56] In *Embattled Paradise: The American Family in an Age of Uncertainty*, the sociologist Arlene Skolnick describes how the combined effects of the GI Bill's educational and housing benefits went far beyond Americans' acquiring skills and buying houses and appliances. The new middle class also attended concerts, went to museums and libraries, and bought books and magazines. This was a new kind of middle class and a new kind of consumer economy.

That Social Security, Medicare, and the 1944 GI Bill worked does not mean these government policies were perfect. Both Social Security and the GI Bill enhanced institutional racism. Social Security benefits were excluded for agricultural and domestic workers, who in 1935 included a substantial proportion of African-American men and women. In the 1940s, the military was segregated, and the GI Bill's benefits reached a limited number of African-American men and women. And, of course, both Social Security and Medicare have financial issues and face the continuing threat of running out of funds.

These and other limitations and problems notwithstanding, the three government policies were able to deliver significant social benefits without creating a lumbering and inefficient federal or state bureaucracy. The "voucher" approach to GI educational benefits, which gave the funding directly to the veterans and not to colleges and universities, was consistent with a "market approach" to social policy. Moreover, these programs, even with their limitations, have been considered "fair" for more than seventy years. Millionaires and manual laborers receive Social Security and Medicare benefits because both contributed to funding them during their working careers. On the other hand, no one met the veterans at the docks in 1945 and means-tested them for the educational and housing benefits offered by the GI Bill. Rich and poor had served their country equally and were entitled to the benefits a grateful nation bestowed on them.

Chapter 4

EFFECTIVE GOVERNMENT SOCIAL PROGRAMS: A NEW BLUEPRINT

Government has struggled for years to create policies that help needy citizens, and as we have seen, contrary to the third lie, it does sometimes hit the bull's eye. Successful programs have at least three things in common. First, they are universal, that is, they provide for a specified population without a means test or some form of complex targeting; second, they have a minimum eligibility test, like serving in the military or turning a specific age; and third, they require relatively small bureaucracies to support them.

These characteristics form a template that can be used as a blueprint for new programs that work. To some, this blueprint might seem like code for another "big government" program. I do not accept this argument. Government becomes too big and unwieldy not simply because too much money is spent. Big (and bad) government means a big bureaucracy whose main function is to determine who gets what, when, and for how long. It is not simply the money that leads to ineffective government; it is the creation of a large infrastructure whose main function is to determine eligibility.

PREVIOUS PROPOSALS

In creating this blueprint, I am building on the important work of others. As Isaac Newton famously said, "If I have seen further it is by standing on ye shoulders of Giants."[1] While my forerunners may not be "giants" in the sense Newton meant, they have provided valuable insights and information that have greatly aided me in formulating my own proposals.

A Child/Family Allowance

In 1986, social policy scholars Irwin Garfinkel and Sara McLanahan examined the problem of single-parent families in their book *Single*

Mothers and Their Children: A New American Dilemma.[2] They focused on the fact that children raised by single parents—primarily mothers whose incomes fell below the poverty line—faced numerous problems. The findings were not particularly surprising, given that the mother's poverty, and not just her being single, was the factor mainly responsible for the children's deficits, which included school problems, delinquent behavior, and emotional difficulties. However, the authors came up with a unique policy to deal with the poverty of single mothers and its impact on their children. They proposed doing away with the dependent child exemption in the Internal Revenue Code (which was $1080 in 1984) and replacing it with *a universal $300 to $400 child allowance payment to all parents of dependent children*. In addition, Garfinkel and McLanahan proposed a $300 to $400 adult allowance paid to all adults in the United States. The logic behind the adult allowance was to reduce the financial advantage of being a parent and possibly of having children out of marriage.

It is hard to see how $300 to $400 per year would be such a powerful incentive to have children. The logic was that the child allowance policy would not require significant additional federal funding; that poor mothers never received the advantage of the dependent exemption because their income was too low to be taxed in the first place; and finally, that the marginal utility of the $300 to $400 payment would be far greater for poor single mothers compared to other recipients of the payments.

Garfinkel and McLanahan's proposal failed to gain any traction; in fact, I may be the only person who resonated with their idea and cited it in my own writings. This failure was due, in minor part, to the proposal's presentation in an academic book, the main focus of which was not policy, but a rigorous scientific analysis of the results of being raised by a single parent. A second, much more important, limitation was that in their proposal the payments would be made to adults, including single mothers with children. This raised the specter of poor parents misusing the money ("They would buy drugs or Cadillacs") and of single mothers getting an incentive to have more children out of marriage, since they would get more money for each child born. Concerns like this always limit support for residual or universal programs that attempt to help children but provide the payments to parents.

Finally, the entire topic of single parenthood became a political lightning rod a few years after the publication of Garfinkel and McLanahan's book. In 1992, then Vice President Dan Quayle sparked a media frenzy when he criticized a television character for choosing to be a single parent. In a speech to the Commonwealth Club of California on the subject of the Los Angeles riots, Quayle blamed the violence on a decay of moral values and family structure in American society. Then, as an aside, he said: "It doesn't help matters when primetime TV has Murphy Brown, a character who supposedly epitomizes today's intelligent, highly paid professional woman, mocking the importance of fathers by bearing a child alone and calling it just another lifestyle choice."[3]

At that point, those who believed choosing to be a single parent was a legitimate lifestyle choice wanted no part of scientific research that supported the idea that children raised by single parents were disadvantaged. On the other hand, if anyone argued that the problem was poverty and not single parenthood, there would be little public acceptance for supporting this lifestyle choice with federal funds. So, in the end, Garfinkel and McLanahan's idea remained quietly unnoticed in the back pages of their book.

Social welfare scholar Duncan Lindsey also saw merit in providing a form of universal support for children. In two editions of his *The Welfare of Children*,[4] Lindsey examined the relationship between poverty and child maltreatment. He concluded that sixty years of policies and programs had failed to address meaningfully the problem of child abuse and neglect in the United States. Lindsey argued that the reason for this failure was that the underlying cause of child maltreatment—economic disadvantage—was not being addressed.

Lindsey reviewed a number of plausible social programs and then, at the end of his book(s), he proposed a form of Social Security program for children. Among his proposals is a "universal children's allowance" such as those implemented in more than seventy nations, including most of Western Europe and Canada.[5] Belgium, for example, instituted its children's allowance in 1944 and provides parents with an annual benefit of $933 for the first child and $793 for the second. The program is not means-tested and the allowance is given to all parents. Norway's program is the most generous children's allowance benefit in the world, with a non-means-tested allowance of $3,536 for each child. In some countries, such as Canada, the government taxes the allowance. In a graduated income tax system the government gets back some of the monies from the more well-to-do recipients.

Lindsey went on to note that similar proposals had been made in the United States. Yale Law School professors Bruce Ackermann and Anne Alstott proposed a one-time grant of $80,000 for each child when he or she reaches the age of eighteen.[6] The young adult could access no more than $20,000 per year and would have to pay the grant back. The expectation was that the grant would be paid back, with interest, at the time of death—a form of estate tax that would amount to about $250,000.

Lindsey's own approach in *The Welfare of Children* is a "child's future security account" into which the federal government would deposit $1,000 at birth and $500 in subsequent years until the child reaches the age of eighteen. Parents would select a registered brokerage firm with which to invest the funds, and they could also add to the fund if they chose—much like the current Internal Revenue Service Section 529 plan that allows parents or relatives to invest for college savings. The accumulated funds would be available to children when they turn eighteen. Lindsey suggests that the funds could be withdrawn at age eighteen or later for education and other investments in one's future, but could not be used for consumer items—electronic equipment, automobiles, clothing, etc.

In his 2008 book, *Child Poverty and Inequality: Securing a Better Future for America's Children*,[7] Lindsey proposes universal income security policies that would benefit vulnerable children and families, strategies that have worked in other advanced democracies and that also respect the importance of the market economy. While the policy would be universal, the intended goal would be to reduce child poverty. Beyond assisting poor children, the universal nature of the policy would also give all children meaningful economic opportunity. Just as Social Security alleviates the sting of poverty in old age, asset-building policies can insulate children from the cumulative effects of disadvantage and provide them with a strong foundation.

Like Garfinkel and McLanahan's 1986 proposal, Lindsey's universalistic solution to the problems of disadvantaged children failed to garner attention or find support in the policy arena. Again, this may be because the proposal comes at the end of an academic book and focuses on a detailed examination of child maltreatment. Whatever the reason, Lindsey's book failed to ignite a discussion of universalistic policies for children. In my heart I hoped it would, but burying the proposal in a book called *Child Poverty and Inequality*, which received little publicity and few reviews, did not help it attract bipartisan attention.

Even though Lindsey's ideas have not gained much public notice, legislation similar to his proposal has been introduced by the United States Congress. The America Saving for Personal Investment, Retirement, and Education Act (ASPIRE) was initially sponsored by former Senator and former Governor of New Jersey, John Corzine, a Democrat, and by former Pennsylvania Senator Rick Santorum, a Republican. The bill was proposed first in the 108th Congress (2003–2004), and it has been proposed in each of the past four Congresses. ASPIRE legislation calls for a deposit of $500 for every newborn in the United States. The funds in the account would compound over time. When the child would reach the age of eighteen the money could be used for education, home ownership, or later for retirement. Additional funds up to $500 would be deposited each year by the federal government to match funds in the account by parents, states, foundations, or other entities. For children in families below the national median income ($50,303 in 2008), an additional $500 would be deposited at the time of birth.

The ASPIRE funds would be managed by parents or guardians, and the managers could make decisions about how the funds should be invested (unlike Social Security). Between the ages of eighteen and twenty-four a recipient could only withdraw funds for post-secondary education; the withdrawn funds would be transferred directly to the educational institution. After the age of twenty-five, the funds could be used for home purchases and retirement. ASPIRE was introduced again in the 111th Congress after September 2009, and was sponsored by a bipartisan coalition of senators and members of the House of Representatives. The bill failed to move beyond introduction, as the debate over health care dominated congressional activity from September 2009 into 2010. The bill will likely be introduced in the 112th Congress, although the current economic conditions and the enormous federal deficit make it unlikely the bill will become law.

Another attempt at crafting a universal policy for children came during Hillary Clinton's presidential campaign. In September 2007, candidate Clinton floated the idea of a $5,000 "baby bond." Clinton was quoted as saying, "I like the idea of giving every baby born in America a $5,000 account that will grow over time, so when that young person turns eighteen, if they have finished high school they will be able to access it to go to college, or maybe they will be able to put that down payment on their first home, or go into business."[8]

Prior to this presentation to the Congressional Black Caucus, Senator Clinton had proposed a $500 baby bond. With the assumption that the bond would not be retroactive, the initial cost, assuming 4 million births per year in the United States, would be $20 billion. But the idea was merely a trial balloon. Senator Clinton never fleshed out how the compounding would be done, never considered whether children already alive would be eligible, and never provided details on how the program could be funded. The New America Foundation, which had worked with Senator Clinton on the concept of the baby bond, did follow up on this idea and is a prime promoter of ASPIRE. Even with Hillary Clinton out of the Senate the baby bond idea still survives in the form of the ASPIRE legislation.

Asset Building

The contemporary "giant" whose ideas have gained the most attention is Michael Sherraden, Benjamin E. Youngdahl Professor of Social

Development at the Washington University, George Warren Brown School of Social Work. Sherraden approaches poverty from an "asset building" rather than "family allowance" perspective. In his 1991 book *Assets and the Poor: A New American Welfare Policy*,[9] Sherraden proposed establishing individual savings accounts for the poor, also known as Individual Development Accounts (IDAs). His program calls for the government and private sector to match individual contributions to IDAs as a means of encouraging savings and breaking the cycle of poverty. IDAs can be used for homeownership, education, small business, or other development purposes. IDAs have been adopted in federal legislation, such as the Community Reinvestment Act (PL 95-128), and in more than forty states, and are the idea behind the ASPIRE legislation. Individual Development Accounts do not have to be reserved only for the poor. Sherraden reminded me in a personal communication that IDAs were originally proposed in 1991 as universal, progressive accounts beginning as early as birth.

FOUNDATIONS OF GOOD SOCIAL POLICY

With the exception of the Individual Development Accounts, the proposals I have been describing did not fly, but they contained the kernels of good ideas. By and large, they were either trial balloons (Senator Clinton) or sidebar solutions tacked on to books that examined social problems. To date, and to the best of my knowledge, such proposals have never been the "raison d'être" for a book. ASPIRE, which is part universal and part means-tested, is the closest attempt at crafting a supportive social policy, but the investment of $500 per child is not sufficient to make a significant impact. Individual Development Accounts promote asset building, but the amount of assets built still remains relatively modest.

I believe that in order for a policy proposal to be meaningful, it needs to be based on a foundation of principles and assumptions that are logical, supported by scientific evidence (if available), and financially sound. Five principles and assumptions underlie my proposal:

1. The Policy Must Direct Resources Directly to the Children.

If sixty years of means-tested welfare support have taught us anything, it is that policymakers and the American public will not support legislation that provides a guaranteed entitlement to poor parents in the hope of upgrading their children's life chances. Many people still endorse the unsubstantiated belief that poor parents will use the money intended to help their children to buy drugs or fancy cars rather than to improve the lot of their children. Programs such as children's allowances, which have been around in Western Europe for more than seven decades, are not going to happen in the United States, because the funds go to parents. Any program that does not provide direct funds to children will not gain sufficient public or political support for implementation.

2. The Policy Must Be Universal—No Means-Testing. Everyone Is Eligible.

Historically, *the few universal social policies that government has put into place have been successful*—e.g., the GI Bill, Medicare, and Social Security. In contrast, residual social policies have been far less successful in providing real broad-based help. The core problem is setting the criteria to determine who will be eligible for government support, how much support will they be eligible for, and for how long. The implementation of the Individuals with Disabilities Education Act (IDEA) in Hawaii as a result of "Felix versus Waihee" is a dramatic example of all that can go wrong with a well-intended residual policy. The state definition of who would be eligible for a free and appropriate education in the least restrictive environment created so much ambiguity that the rolls of eligible children expanded dramatically during the course of the lawsuit. Parents, teachers, and counselors fought to include children as "deserving" of special education services.

Among the likely reasons ASPIRE has never been enacted is that the additional $500 for children in homes with income below the national median is a bit of a poison pill, because this provision requires creating a government agency to administer the distribution of the additional $500. The new government agency, rightly or wrongly, signals "bigger government."

Child maltreatment is a second problem that still struggles with eligibility issues. The number of child abuse reports grew exponentially in the first decade after the federal government enacted the Child Abuse Prevention and Treatment Act in 1974. Professionals and laypersons alike followed mandatory reporting requirements in a well-intentioned effort to bring services and protection to maltreated children. When, after more than a decade of increasing reports, it became evident that reporting did not directly lead to greater safety for maltreated children or help for the offenders, the number and rate of reporting flattened out and actually fell in 2008–2009.

In the case of child maltreatment, recipients of government assistance were often reluctant to accept a helping hand. Parents and caregivers recoiled at being labeled "child abusers" and they resisted help because that would mean admitting to abuse or neglect. In my own experience, few families who are investigated for suspected child abuse and neglect welcome the investigator or the proffered helping hand. Suspected maltreaters see child protective services workers as "baby snatchers" and resist giving any information that could lead to their children's being taken away. And while some children are relieved to be removed from abusive homes, many more actively oppose being taken from their parents—no matter what their parents have done.

Social safety-net programs are obviously the best example of the failure of government residual social policies. Identifying the "deserving poor" and setting amounts and time lengths for assistance consume a great deal of time and energy. A major safety-net program, Aid to Families with Dependent Children, shifted in 1996 from open-ended entitlements to block grants to states. The shift from AFDC to TANF, Temporary Assistance to Needy Families, was accompanied by rigorous eligibility rules as well as time limits on how long welfare recipients would be eligible for support. In the decade after welfare reform, the official rate of those receiving welfare payments declined. Thus, the goal of the new welfare legislation was accomplished—welfare rolls decreased. There was additional federal funding for child care and job training, but the issue of whether the program provided an adequate safety net and improved the life chances of children was never addressed, as that was not the actual intent of the legislation.

The debates about eligibility and about the bureaucracy required to determine the "bright lines," the thresholds at which people are eligible for residual benefits, dissipate much of government's good intentions. The end result is frustrated policymakers, a disillusioned public, and minimal aid to the truly disadvantaged. The solution is to devise a policy that serves as a lever placed beneath the center of gravity of the social problem, and to use the lever to raise the entire issue rather than simply chipping away at the edges. Universal programs have demonstrated their effectiveness as such levers.

3. The Policy Must Be *Fair*—No One Is Left Out.

Efforts to help the needy are almost always wrapped in high-minded ideological principles. Terms like equity, equality, and social justice are inadequate for a number of reasons. First and foremost, there is actually little public support for equity and equality in a market-driven economy. Most people agree that citizens should have equitable access to education and economic opportunities. But this merely means that everyone should get to the starting line at the same time. Few people support giving some runners extra help when the gun goes off. Income redistribution as a social policy enjoys little support in a market economy. For example, by the end of the 2008 presidential campaign the most consistent criticisms leveled against Barack Obama was that if elected, he would redistribute wealth in the United States. Some of the negative responses to the president's proposals for health care reform are based on beliefs that income redistribution is the hidden agenda of that reform.

The policies and programs that enjoy widespread support are those that are considered fair. The social policy doctrine of fairness has been developed and advanced by the sociologist Amatai Etzioni and his colleagues, who support the values of communitarianism.[10] In this small book, I cannot do justice to the theoretical formulations of communitarianism, but Etzioni attempts to capture it in his "new golden rule": *"Respect and uphold society's moral order as you would have society respect and uphold your autonomy."*[11]

Etzioni struggles to find a common ground to attract liberals and conservatives to the new golden rule. Fairness—which he notes is "a value that appears to most people as 'self-evident truth'"—is one of his key concepts.[12] A fair society, according to Etzioni,

> has strong political appeal because of its universality. In this sense, it is similar to popular Medicare (compared to Medicaid) and to Social Security (compared to welfare). Policies that help the disadvantaged catch up can be accommodated with a fairness doctrine as long as they are framed appropriately. Thus instead of reiterating the outrage—and an outrage it is—that there are 44 million Americans with no health insurance, fairness calls for everyone to be covered.[13]

In June 2004, Etzioni submitted his propositions to an empirical test. He commissioned a poll with a random sample of one thousand likely voters. From this sample, five hundred respondents were asked to respond to seven social policies and say whether each was "very fair," "fair," "unfair," or "very unfair." The first point stated: "Millions of American workers spent their entire careers with one company on the basis of a contract that promised them a pension plan to provide for them and their families in retirement, only to have the company cut their pension and benefits after they retired." Nearly six out of ten (58 percent) of those questioned thought this policy was very unfair. The second point stated: "Health insurance companies have avoided paying an insured person's bills when costly illnesses occur even after that person has fully paid health insurance premiums for years." Nearly two out of three respondents (64 percent) thought this policy was "very unfair."

The questions went on to ask about federal deficits, Internal Revenue Service audits, salaries of CEOs of large corporations, tax breaks, and the Patriot Act, which was enacted after 9/11.

After presenting the seven questions, Etzioni gave respondents a definition of a fair society as one in which "nobody is left behind; anyone who seeks work can get a job; nobody is cheated out of his or her pension rights, and health care is accessible to everyone."[14] When asked if they would vote for a candidate who supported such a fair society, more than half of those surveyed said they would be "much more likely" to "somewhat more likely" to support such a candidate. Finally, the survey demonstrated the broad demographics of those who supported a "fair society." Support came from men and women across age groups; Democrats, Republicans, and Independents; liberals, moderates, and conservatives.

In conclusion, Etzioni states that his survey demonstrates a widespread support of policies that are perceived to be fair. Fairness, however, is only one principle. Etzioni believes it only fair that all Americans have access to health care. He does not, however, ask questions about the affordability of health care, which to some people is a much greater issue. Moreover, the private insurance companies that would cease to exist if there were a national universal health insurance have fought, and continue to fight, against such a proposal. Fairness is a necessary principle, but it is an entirely insufficient precept on which to base a universal social policy.

4. The Policy Must Be Fundable. The Proposal Must Include a Realistic Method of Funding.

Social activists, myself included, tend to propose programs without considering costs or sources of funding. When we do consider these factors, we assume that the proposal has so much moral value that the money will be found somewhere. Or we make comparisons that we hope will induce enough guilt to persuade policymakers to transfer monies from one program to another, as if there were no separation of powers in government.

My own early folly was to compare federal spending on child abuse and neglect prevention programs to military spending. I once opined during testimony before a House Committee that the entire federal budget for preventing child maltreatment was the equivalent of the cost of one new jet fighter.[15] Who could argue against such logic—prevent child abuse by building one less fighter plane? It never happened.

A colleague of mine, using a slightly different tack, explained that the entire national child welfare budget—including federal, state, and county expenditures—was smaller than what Americans spend on pizza each year. I never looked up the pizza statistic, but I assume my colleague could support his claim. Of course, like my fighter plane example, this comparison is irrelevant and useless. First, child welfare funding is spent on no more than 2 million children, while some 200 million people eat pizza every year. Second, it seems unlikely that Americans will suddenly stop eating pizza and send the saved money to agencies that strive to prevent child abuse. And third, well, the comparison is just silly.

A major underlying question about what is fundable is, "What is affordable?" Are the wars against Iraq and Afghanistan "affordable"? If a bank or an insurance company is considered "too big to fail," are billions of dollars in government bailout money "affordable"? Is an economic stimulus bill in a deep recession "affordable"? These are not budgetary questions; they are questions about values, beliefs, and priorities.

I cannot resolve a debate over what is affordable. My straightforward point is that for a proposal to be acceptable it must include a defendable means to fund the policy *now*; projected savings in the future are not sufficient. Hillary Clinton's "baby bond" idea would have cost $20 billion. Where would that money have come from? Lindsey, Garfinkel, and McLanahan included in their proposals a mechanism to offset the cost of the programs they proposed. They would have funded their child and adult allowances by converting the then $2,000 child exemption for parents in the Internal Revenue Code from a $300 tax savings to a $400 benefit (depending on tax bracket). The offset would create the program with no additional costs or taxes.

The bottom line is simple. Calculate the cost of the program and find a budget offset to fund it. Do not play accounting games and fund the program with hypothesized future savings.

5. The Program Has to Be Consistent with the Values and Principles of a Market Economy.

On the surface, the battleground of social policies appears to be Democrats versus Republicans or liberals versus conservatives. In my opinion, the true battle is between those who believe in the principles and virtues of a market economy and those who believe that a society should create and fund programs that benefit all segments of the population (in other words, socialism).

A long forgotten, but poignant example of this battle occurred during the second term of Richard Nixon's administration. Building on Lyndon Johnson's War on Poverty, in 1971 the Democrat-controlled Senate passed a bill entitled The Comprehensive Child Development Act.[16] The bill was sponsored by Walter Mondale, who would run for president in 1984, and Indiana Representative John Brademas, who would go on to become president of New York University. The Mondale-Brademas bill was designed to establish a comprehensive system of childcare. It was also an attempt to deal with the shortcomings of the American welfare system, as embodied in the residual policy of Aid to Families with Dependent Children.

The welfare situation was an important part of the history of the act, since childcare legislation would alleviate welfare problems by providing quality care for children so that their mothers could work. As amended, the Comprehensive Child Development Act ended up being another residual social policy, as government funding would not be extended to either all working mothers or all children. The legislation would provide free daycare services for families with incomes below $4,320 per year (for a family of four), while allowing other families to pay on a sliding scale.[17]

The bill was passed by both the House and Senate. But on December 9, 1971, President Nixon vetoed the legislation, criticizing its "fiscal irresponsibility, administrative unworkability [sic], and family-weakening implications." Such direct federal provision of daycare services, he charged, "would commit the vast moral authority of the National Government to the side of communal approaches to child rearing over against the family-centered approach."[18]

Although often attributed to President Nixon's veto message, the strongest criticism of the Comprehensive Child Development Act came from the late columnist James K. Kilpatrick, who said that the enactment of the bill would "Sovietize American youth."[19] Kilpatrick's quote was especially ironic in 2008, when the federal government committed nearly a trillion dollars to buy and support major financial institutions such as Freddie Mac and Fannie Mae, thus "Sovietizing" the American financial system.

"Sovietize" and "Communist" have just about disappeared from the American political vocabulary. With the end of the Cold War, and the rise of the perceived threat of Islamic terrorists, one can no longer use a Red Scare tactic to defeat legislation. That said, the traditional battle between a market-based economy and socialism still lurks beneath the surface of any social legislation. Anyone proposing new comprehensive social programs would be wise not to forget the lesson of the demise of the Comprehensive Child Development Act of 1971. It is clear that America is not ready for social policies that would be interpreted as the transfer of wealth and assets from the rich to the poor.

What are the key components of social policies that follow market economy principles? I offer a few basic tenets:

- Policies that encourage asset building are preferable to policies that merely transfer assets from the well-to-do to the deserving poor. Individual Development Accounts are preferable to baby bonds or children's allowances.
- Policies that incentivize are more effective than policies that merely meet needs. Microfinancing to help spur economic enterprise would be preferable to welfare programs.
- Policies that enhance and reward deferred gratification—such as investing in a college or technical education—are more effective than policies that require the recipient to consume all resources in order to meet basic needs.
- Policies should not be perceived to support behaviors and actions that a wide segment of the population believes to be inappropriate or harmful (even if the perception is inaccurate). Increasing benefits for welfare recipients who have an additional child is meant not to punish the innocent child, but such a policy enjoys very little support as it seems to encourage women to have children they cannot afford. Another example was articulated by one of my former students who was appalled to find that families who qualified for fixed-cost home heating under a City of Philadelphia program kept their thermostats at 70 degrees. The justification offered by the recipients of the means-tested program—"Well, we only pay a fixed amount so why not keep the house warm?"
- Policies that lead to more consumers and a better prepared workforce will win more support than policies that merely help people. The rationale for extending the Bush-era tax cuts at the end of 2010 was that taxes saved by the wealthy would help stimulate the economy. No one argued that extending unemployment benefits (a provision in the same legislation) would do anything more than support the disadvantaged.
- Policies that require means-testing or determining who is deserving are inferior to policies that do not require installing a new or larger government agency. The examples I have used throughout the first three chapters of this book support this principle.

There may well be more principles and details that apply to the policy I propose, but in the end it will be the policy, and not the scaffolding, that merits the most complete and careful discussion.

The Goal and "Face" of the Policy

There are two more principles that must be met for an effective government policy. First and most important is the goal of the program. What exactly is it designed to fix? The second, a more emotional principle, is the program's "face." Who do we envision will be helped by the program? What does that person look like today and what will he or she look like when the program succeeds?

What to Fix?

The first question, "What is the goal?" turns out to be more complex than it seems. What should we fix? When I selected the story of Jennifer Felix as an example of a failed government effort, I assumed the effort's goal to be "meeting the needs of disadvantaged children," and the "face" to be those children and their families. Two constraints loomed over the goal, as well as my purported "face." First, most programs designed to assist the poor and disadvantaged end up being residual and non-universal, and, as I have argued, these programs frequently fail because the bloated bureaucracy and game-playing of the means test erode their funding and thwart their intent. The second constraint is the difficulty to get the assistance directly to the children without going through their parents and caregivers. This constraint is key not because I don't trust parents, especially poor and disadvantaged parents, but because I am convinced it is impossible to generate political support for a program in which the funding flows through the parents. I am numbed by the prospect of hearing advocates and politicians claim the parents will just use the money for drugs or squander it on luxury purchases. While I know empirically that this is just a canard, I also know it will block any proposal that allocates funding through parents. I believe this is why the United States has never adopted or even carefully considered "baby bonds" or "social security for children."

I am left with the realization that if I want to help children—and especially disadvantaged children—I will have to develop a program that becomes available to them when they are adults, and also gives them hope, motivation, and assurance of a future.

What then needs to be fixed? What should the goal be? Oddly enough, as I pondered this question while writing this book, the American economy began to nose-dive. A mortgage crisis morphed into a financial crisis, which morphed into a credit crisis, which led to a massive decline in the stock markets, which then moved the country into a recession, which now manifests itself in tight credit markets, a massive decline in consumer spending, and staggering increases in unemployment. As I began the first draft of this chapter, in 2008, an unemployment rate of 10 percent seemed unimaginable. But it became a reality in a matter of months.

I am not an economist. It took me a while to learn what a credit default swap is, and I still understand only the basics about financial derivatives. So my analysis of where we are, how we got here, and where we need to go is one of an observant social scientist. This is what I see:

- The poverty rate has not changed much in the United States in the last thirty years. The rate has fluctuated from a high of about 15 percent of the population to a low of 11.3 percent. The poverty rate stood at 14.3 percent in 2009. The high point of the number of people in poverty was 40 million in 1993, and the 2008 figure before the country went into recession was 39.8 million.[20]

- Some people have moved into poverty, some people have moved out of poverty, and some people remain poor. In the current recession, more people will become poor and more people will have a difficult time rising out of poverty. The poor had no hand in the current economic problems. When the crisis is over, they will be just as disadvantaged as they have always been, and they will still amount to some 40 million people.

- Much of the outcry and public pain about the current economic climate has come from the well-to-do. One had to actually have a retirement account or stock investments to be impacted by a 4,000-point drop in the Dow Jones average. The poor and the middle class were not directly affected by Bernard Madoff's $50 billion Ponzi scheme. Many well-to-do are much less well-to-do today than two years ago. And a good number of them have found all their assets wiped out. Although the failure of the financial and housing markets and complex financial and investment schemes may have precipitated the recession, the well-to-do is not the group that needs help or for whom programs should be developed. Of course, the government has done exactly that—putting nearly $2 trillion into the economy under the banner of "Troubled Assets Relief Program" (TARP) and committing additional billions of dollars to the American Recovery and Reinvestment Act. In December 2010, Congress extended the Bush-era tax cuts (along with an extension of unemployment coverage). But the rich have done pretty well in the last three decades. In 1981 the share of wealth held by the top 1 percent of people in the United States was 24.8 percent. By 2009 this figure had grown to 35.6 percent.[21]

- The problems of the well-to-do did trickle or in some cases cascade down onto the poor and those at risk of becoming poor. Declining retail sales and housing starts resulted in the loss of jobs and the closing of businesses.
- The government did provide funding that directly helped those with low incomes. Unemployment insurance was extended another twelve months in December 2010 (through the end of 2011), and the American Recovery and Reinvestment Act of 2009 (PL 111-5) allocated billions of dollars in funding that either preserved existing jobs or stimulated the creation of new jobs. Nonetheless, by the middle of 2011 the unemployment rate was still near 10 percent and even higher in especially hard-hit states and communities.

So, if the poor have stayed poor, and the rich have gotten richer (at least until 2008), who has been squeezed in the last thirty years? The answer is clear: *the working class and the middle class*, who have had to struggle to keep up their standard of living. Rising costs of housing and goods and services have not been met by real wage increases for working- and middle-class men and women. What has kept the middle and the working classes afloat has been:

- *Two-worker families*. It has been more than thirty years since a single wage earner could support a family. Single wage-earner homes have the greatest risk of being poor or slipping into poverty.
- *Credit card debt*. In January 2007, Elizabeth Warren, then Harvard Law School professor and currently head of the steering committee of the Federal Consumer Financial Protection Bureau, testified before the U.S. Senate Committee on Banking, Housing and Urban Affairs, declaring that the United States credit card market was broken.[22] Her argument was that consumers can't possibly understand credit card agreements and often find themselves trapped under the weight of 19 percent interest rates. Warren was right on the mark. Moreover, consumers are trapped because their consumption was made not with earnings or savings, but with credit. With no increase in real earning power, the middle and the working classes created, with the generous assistance of the credit card companies, a Ponzi scheme of their own, which was bound to collapse.
- *Home equity debt*. Rising real estate values turned the American home into a seemingly bottomless piggy bank. As housing prices rose, the perceived value of homes went up, and homeowners were encouraged to "use" their home equities. The assumption was that the debt would go away when the home was sold and profit from the sale

would pay off the loan balance. Of course, there were multiple flaws and traps in the model. First, it depended on home values *always* rising. Second, the homeowner would pay off the mortgage and home equity debt upon selling the home, but the net cash from the sale would not produce enough money to purchase another home—as much of the equity would go to paying off the home equity loan. Thus, home values had to rise faster than the consumer would spend the money. Once the music stopped and home values fell, so did the house of cards of perceived wealth.

The real victims in the current economic crisis are the working and the middle classes. They have had to walk away from homes, and they have had to curtail spending. In doing so, they have ground the consumer economy to a screeching halt. Bankruptcies and layoffs in the consumer sector are the direct result of working- and middle-class families giving up their working- or middle-class lifestyle (or what they perceive to be that style) and hunkering down just to survive.

The "Face": It's Main Street

The post-2008 economic crisis lays out in bold relief who has the problem and what needs to be fixed. If there will be a revitalized consumer economy, if children will have a future, if the United States will regain economic health, it will come by rebuilding America's working and middle classes. The recovery will have to occur on Main Street, not on Wall Street.

Although I began this project struggling to identify a policy that would benefit disadvantaged children, I end up proposing that the "face" of the problem is the working and the middle class, not the hungry, homeless, or disadvantaged child. The principles I lay out and the assessment of past programs point to the need to revitalize and support Main Street. It will be Main Street that creates the jobs and opportunities that benefit the poor and those at risk of being poor. And, equally important, it is the aspiration and commitment to live on Main Street that can directly benefit all children.

Chapter 5

REBUILDING MAIN STREET: THE FUTURES ACCOUNT

Government can rebuild Main Street. Government can implement a social policy that will sustain a working and middle class. Government can provide a viable future for America's children.

Rebuilding Main Street requires both looking back at history and looking toward the future. Looking back, we see that the most effective social program was the GI Bill. As described in Chapter 3, it allowed returning soldiers (albeit, mostly white males) to advance their education and, at the same time, invest in the American dream of home ownership. The bill increased the skills and analytic abilities of countless veterans, since the core of a college education, the liberal arts, is designed to enhance critical thinking and analytic ability. Higher education also gave the returning veterans the opportunity for intensive study in science, quantitative reasoning, and preprofessional curricula in law, medicine, social service, and business.

Advanced education provided a second benefit: it gentrified the population. College provides opportunities to experience literature and the arts. College graduates continue reading, attending concerts and plays, and exploring music and the fine arts. Patronage of the arts and libraries increased rapidly after World War II, due to the increase in the number of college graduates.

At the heart of the GI Bill were mortgages that allowed returning soldiers to purchase homes at affordable interest rates. There is absolutely nothing like home ownership to stimulate consumer spending—on appliances, construction materials, tools, paint, and an endless supply of consumer goods. Every home purchase—from a new wastepaper basket to a stove or freezer—stimulates the economy. And home upkeep is an ongoing stimulus.

Homes are money pits for the owners and engines of progress for the economy. But individuals and families who cannot afford a home, who lose a home to foreclosure, or who are insecure about their economic present and future, disinvest—willingly or unwillingly—in home ownership and upkeep. Nothing can bring an economy to a sudden parade rest more quickly than disinvestment in home ownership. If I fear I am going to lose my home or if I know I cannot sell it, I will disinvest. If I worry about putting food on the table and meeting other needs, I will disinvest. When millions of people disinvest, the economy grinds to a halt—as we saw at the end of 2008 and through 2010.

The working and the middle classes are not just about the present—getting an education and owning a home. It is about the future. Many people aspire to the Main Street lifestyle, which includes home ownership and enough education to assure job security. Unfortunately, that lifestyle is unattainable without an education and sufficient resources for a down payment on a home. And if enough people give up aspiring to join the middle class, if education and home ownership become far out of reach, it is likely that wide segments of the population will give up aspiring to the dream. Giving up the goal of social advancement—at least as far as gaining membership in the middle class—can quickly lead to alienation. If you are not going to go to college and if a high school diploma is insufficient to assure economic advancement, why even bother to finish high school? If the symbols of adulthood—education, a secure job, and home ownership—are unattainable, one can at least signify adult status by becoming a parent, in or outside of marriage.

I will forgo the full literature review on poverty, deviance, and out-of-marriage parenthood, and simply point out that people are willing to defer present gratification when they have a reasonable chance at future gratification. If the road to education, homeownership, material possessions, and life security is blocked, only the most persistent and resilient will push through the constraints. The rest will invest in the present and give up the future.

Without a secure middle class, stimulus packages, tax cuts, short-term job programs, and stronger safety nets will not rebuild and solidify Main Street. Without a strong middle class, the United States' economic outlook is dire. To rebuild a true Main Street that will support a consumer market economy, government policy has to look in the long term at building and securing a future. Toward that end, I propose a program that would offer the opportunity for higher education and homeownership to every child born in the United States. The goals and features of the "Futures Account" are more substantial and more universal than any of the policies I have been describing up to now.

The Futures Account

The Futures Account builds on the work of Michael Sherraden and his concept of Individual Development Accounts. However, it is based on the five principles articulated in the previous chapter: that is, it is universal and is not just an antipoverty program. The amounts are considerably larger that Sherraden's IDAs, and its use is more strictly limited.

Here are the five main characteristics of the proposed Futures Account.

1. The Account

The Futures Account would be universal, available to every child born in the United States or who is a legal resident of the United States. The account would be opened with the application and receipt of the child's Social Security number. When he or she reaches the age of eighteen, access to the account is guaranteed.

There would be no disqualifying factors. Even people incarcerated at the time they turn eighteen would be eligible to access the account for education or housing (obviously, at a later date). People who are not mentally capable of making decisions would have a guardian appointed to allocate the funds from the account.

2. The Deposit

The actual amount of the Futures Account must be meaningful as an asset. The amount I propose is based on the assumption that $3,000 would be deposited into the account for eighteen years. The account would not generate interest; thus, a child would accumulate $54,000 by the time he or she turns eighteen. In reality, though, there is no yearly accounting. The Futures Account makes the full amount available at age eighteen and, unless an incentivizing formula is added to the account (see below), there is no need for a yearly accrual or accounting. The $54,000 in 2011 dollars would be enough to pay for one year of tuition and fees at an Ivy League or private university or all four years at the University of California, Los Angeles (at the 2010 cost of tuition). This amount would be enough for a 20 percent down payment on a $270,000 home. The U.S. Census Bureau estimated that the median sales price of a home and land in July 2009 was $210,100, while the average was $269,200.

No doubt the amount of the account will prompt considerable debate, should my idea ever move to a legislative proposal. But assuming a $3,000 per year deposit and the costs of housing and education, $54,000 appears to be an appropriate amount to begin with. The Futures Account can be adjusted based on the changing costs of education and housing.

Let's assume the new Futures Account begins with a full payment to the first cohort of those turning eighteen years of age. (In other words, the account would be retroactive and would not require the actual accumulation of assets, as Social Security does.) In 2011, 4.4 million Americans will turn eighteen.[1] In the first year of implementation, the cost of providing the asset of $54,000 to 4.4 million children would be $237 billion. In order to be considered even remotely possible, a Futures Account would require finding a $237 billion offset in current federal spending and in the tax code. More on that later.

3. Withdrawals

Unlike the Social Security Trust Fund, the Futures Account is a real account with an annual defined obligation. The account has to be in a "lock box" because there is a possibility of a $237 billion payout each year. Once a person turns eighteen, he or she will receive an annual statement regarding the payments and balance in the account. The fund is a real obligation: monies raised through taxes in a single year would have to be available to pay the appropriation in the account each year.[2] However, unlike Social Security, there would be no continuing obligation for annual payments, nor would one generation of workers pay for the benefits of a later generation. There would be a Futures Account created for each child in the United States as he or she turns eighteen.

The devil in any proposal to help children has always been that funding must be given to parents or some other guardian—the state, county, or school system. In contrast, the Futures Account is under the sole control of the individual when he or she turns eighteen. At that point, assets can be withdrawn from the account for only two purposes: education and housing. The withdrawal would be accomplished only by electronic transfer to a qualified educational institution or as part of a housing transaction through a lending institution. The funds are, in reality, a form of voucher for education or home ownership.

There would be no survival rights to asset accounts. If an account holder dies prior to his or her eighteenth birthday, the assets would be returned to the U.S. Treasury. If the account holder dies after the age of eighteen, with an unspent, unobligated balance in the account, the remaining funds would be returned to the Treasury.

4. Incentivizing

The Futures Account could also include incentivizing provisions based on a child's specific accomplishments before the age of eighteen. The most significant incentive would be a high-school graduation incentive payment of $5,000. In 2009, 87 percent of adults twenty-five years of age or older in the United States had completed high school.[3] While this is an impressive overall statistic, it still leaves 14 percent without a high-school degree. This is a population exposed to numerous risks, including poverty, a population that lacks a key credential for entry into the skilled workforce. Without unusual talents or accomplishments, those without a high-school diploma are substantially blocked from a Main Street lifestyle and Main Street security.

Moreover, this statistic does not tell the whole story. In 2008, Hispanics between the ages of sixteen and twenty-four had a high school dropout rate of 18.3 percent.[4] In Detroit, only 21.7 percent of students graduated from high school, while in Baltimore the figure is a pitifully small 34.6 percent. In Philadelphia, fewer than half—49.2 percent—of students in urban high schools graduate, compared to more than eight in ten students (82.4 percent) in the Philadelphia suburban high schools.[5] Thus, the problems of educational accomplishment, development of necessary work skills, and possibility of economic growth are far worse in major cities than it is in the rest of the country.

High-school graduation is not the only possible incentive. Not being convicted of a juvenile offense is another. The College Crusade of Rhode Island asks students who enroll to pledge that they will stay in school, avoid trouble with the law, drugs, alcohol, and early parenthood, and be a role model in their community.[6] While the pledge is certainly well intended, it is difficult to monitor, especially since juvenile arrest and conviction records are confidential. Moreover, it opens the door for a cultural and moral debate on out-of-marriage pregnancy. In fact, the program only monitors whether the students graduate from high school and qualify for financial aid on a need basis. In the end, incentivizing high-school graduation seems appropriate and should provoke minimal dissent and debate. What is especially attractive is the ability to incentivize graduation without creating a new bureaucracy.

Another plausible incentive is public service. In the last two decades, high schools, colleges, and universities have increasingly required students to engage in public service. Of course, some of the volunteerism is as much motivated by resume building as by altruism. The problem with encouraging public service is not motivation, but elitism. Those who can "volunteer" are young men and women who can afford to do so.

Even for programs that provide compensation, such as America Corps or Teach for America, the wages are so modest as to exclude many eligible and willing participants. Many fine students who could volunteer or join low-wage programs cannot do so because they must earn money.

To level the playing field a bit, the Futures Account could incentivize public service activities with government organizations or registered human service nonprofits. The incentive should be based on an accumulation of hours (along the lines of banking frequent flyer miles with commercial airlines) or for a year of public service. There have already been proposals to incentivize public service. During the 2008 presidential campaign, both major party candidates discussed incentives for public service. Barack Obama endorsed a payment of $4,000 per year, while Republican candidate John McCain worried that too large a payment might be considered a "bribe." In fact, a $4,000 incentive would be a marginal addition to an existing Futures Account and probably is not a large enough proportion of the account to be thought of as a bribe.

5. Offsets: Paying for the Futures Account

For the Futures Account to become a reality, immediate tax offsets would have to be applied to the federal budget. One could argue forever about the potential long-term cost savings and economic advantages of the Futures Account, but that will not pay one cent of the first year cost.

The obvious offsets are:

a) Eliminate the child exemption from the tax code. For tax year 2010 each taxpayer can deduct $3,650 from his or her income for each dependent child in the home.[7] For simplicity purposes, I am going to use the 2008 figure of $3,500. Assuming a taxpayer was in the 30 percent tax bracket, he or she would save $1,050 in tax payments. Stated another way, by eliminating the child exemption, the government would gain $1,050 per qualifying taxpayer at the 30 percent tax bracket.[8] The quick math does not work here, as not every one of the nearly 75 million children have parents or caregivers in the 30 percent tax bracket, and not all children under eighteen are cared for by parents or caregivers who are obliged to pay taxes. According to the Internal Revenue Service Reports, in 2002 there were 130 million tax returns filed, of which 90.6 million represented taxable returns. The average tax rate was 14 percent. Thus, nearly 70 percent of tax-filers paid an average of 14 percent of their adjusted gross income.[9]

It is necessary to know how many taxpayers claimed a child exemption and for how many children. I have neither the expertise nor the knowledge of IRS data to fully calculate the possible gain in revenue the federal government would receive by eliminating the child dependent exemption. However, a cursory calculation would be:

Number of children under the age of 18 (72 million)

x

$3500

x

14% average marginal tax rate

= a total estimated increase in tax payments of $35,280,000,000 or $35 billion

b) Reduce federal funding for college aid. A second offset would require that the federal government get out of the college financial aid business, although the savings here would be modest. Federal funding for higher education has always been a sacred cow, especially the federal Pell Grant program, which offers need-based grants to low-income undergraduate and certain postbaccalaureate students to promote access to postsecondary education. The budget for fiscal year 2007 for Pell Grants was nearly $14 billion.[10] President Bush's 2009 budget request included $95 billion for grants and loans for some 10.9 million students.[11]

With a Futures Account in place, the Pell Grants, as well as other higher-education grants and loans, along with the bureaucracy that supports them, could be phased out because they would no longer be needed. Other categorical federal fellowship and scholarship support for higher education could also be eliminated, as any means-tested aid would no longer be needed. And again, the savings would also include the elimination of a federal bureaucracy supporting such programs.

I will not expand this chapter by combing through the federal budget to find all the means-tested programs related to education and housing that could be eliminated as a result of the Futures Account. That task can be managed by either the Congressional Research Service, the Office of Management of the Budget, or enlightened think tanks.

While finding nearly $250 billion ($237 billion is my original estimate) in offsets is a challenge, it is not impossible. The allocation of the stimulus and Troubled Asset Relief funds demonstrated that the government knows how to find money when necessary. The real challenge would be convincing legislators that the Futures Account would do a far better job of supporting higher education than the existing means-tested programs. The embedded constituencies, the sacred cow status of the programs, and the ability of the supporters of Pell Grants to point to individual success stories of recipients would put up a staunch barrier to policy change. On the other hand, the growing costs of college and university education and the enormous loans many students accumulate—even with the existence of federal grant programs—suggest there would be considerable support for a federal program that could reduce the debt burden for families and students.

c) Eliminate federal earmarks designed to help children. It is tempting, and probably a good thing, to prick and gore some federal sacred cow programs that are supposed to aid children, particularly the so-called federal earmarks. Billions of dollars are spent annually on such programs, and each has an embedded constituency that would fight vigorously to protect their turf, whether or not it benefits children. In the area of juvenile justice alone there are hundreds of millions of dollars in federal spending—much of the money earmarked or designated by Congress—that provide little empirically measured benefit. My personal choice of the most outrageous example is a program that on the surface seems like a good thing: the National Center for Missing and Exploited Children. The center was created in the aftermath of the kidnapping and slaying of six-year-old Adam Walsh in 1981 (see Chapter 1 for the details of this event). Adam's father, John, became the national face of grieving parents of kidnapped and slain children. He eventually hosted a national television program, "America's Most Wanted," which claims to have successfully helped find and convict killers and kidnappers.

The National Center for Missing and Exploited Children was created in 1984, after the enactment of two federal laws that focused on missing children. In 2009, the total budget for the Center was $48 million, $37 million of which was funded by the federal government.[12] The funding was a sole-source allocation—meaning no other organization was allowed to apply for funding for a center on missing or exploited children. Thus the funding became a yearly no-bid entitlement for the center. The executive director of the center, Ernie Allen, received a salary of $724,363 in 2009.[13]

The cause of missing children is certainly heart-wrenching. The problem has a face—the kidnapped and slain Adam Walsh, Polly Klass, and the still missing Etan Patz. And it has a website well stocked with compelling statistics and stories. But in the end, this is an earmarked program that draws down $37 million per year in federal funding. Yet the FBI estimates that only between 43 and 147 children are kidnapped and killed by strangers each year. The vast majority of missing children are either runaways or children taken as part of parental abductions.[14] Parental abductions are technically kidnappings, but they are not the same in form and consequences as the cases of Adam Walsh, Polly Klass, and Etan Patz. There are numerous other earmarks—including funding for D.A.R.E (Drug Abuse Resistance Education) and Boot Camp programs for juvenile offenders—many of which look worthy on the surface. But such earmarked programs are a cancer that has spread through government over the past two or three decades, and it is a shame that no one in the legislative or executive branch has had the fortitude to excise the malignancy.

d) Institute a value-added tax. When all acceptable program cuts can be identified and agreed upon, Congress and the executive branch can be tested as to whether they are truly willing to commit to the future of America's children. The dreaded "T" word—tax—is the final offset. I would choose the simplest tax, one that has already been implemented in most European Union countries: a value-added tax on luxury goods. There is an underlying logic and elegance to levying a tax on luxury purchases to fund programs for children. Taxing high-end automobiles, yachts, and jewelry would test Americans' values.

WHAT ABOUT FRAUD AND OTHER UNETHICAL PRACTICES?

It would be naive to believe there would be no fraud when the federal government suddenly makes $237 billion available to eighteen-year-olds for the purposes of education and/or housing. The bursting of the housing bubble in 2008 and the massive increase in foreclosures opened the eyes of policymakers, the media, and the public about fraudulent practices in the home mortgage industry, as well as about the great number of people who were persuaded to purchase homes they could not afford. Similarly, there is increasing concern about colleges and universities that enroll students who have government loans and then leave school with an impractical or incomplete education and a large loan debt. Much of the concern about borderline ethical practices in higher education is directed at the for-profit sector. But many experts also claim that, at current costs, higher education even at the bedrock nonprofit and elite institutions is not worth the cost and is not for everyone.[15]

Indeed, a college or university education is not for everyone. However, the Futures Account could also be used for other forms of postsecondary education, including many forms of vocational and paraprofessional education. Or the full funds could be applied to housing. But, with $237 billion available for postsecondary or higher education, some forms of unethical practices are likely to crop up to defraud well-intentioned eighteen-year-olds.

There are other possibilities for fraud in the Futures Account program. Unscrupulous parents could persuade their adult children to purchase a home, and then force their offspring to sell and turn the money over to them. The eighteen-year-old could do the exact same thing—buy and sell the home and pocket the $54,000. Of course, the Futures Account could include a "lock-up" period during which the home could not be resold or, if resold, the $54,000 would have to be returned to the Futures Fund or to the government. Some argue that eighteen-year-olds are not mature enough to invest the funds wisely, and thus could easily waste or lose the money. I reject an "investment supervision" provision because I want to avoid creating a government entity to engage in or oversee such an enterprise. Social Security funds have been allocated for decades without such government supervision. Yes, there are those elderly who make unwise decisions or who are exploited, but that is always going to be part of a free-market economy.

All these arguments are credible. No system could absolutely prevent fraud in the Futures Account policy. But the same arguments were raised when the GI Bill was debated in the 1940s. There must have been soldiers who used their education voucher and incurred debt for higher education that was not helpful. Some homes purchased with GI loans must have been foreclosed. But in the end, the positive results of the program far outweighed anecdotal accounts and concerns about waste and fraud.

I am certain of only two things: 1) Some young men and women will use the Futures Funds unwisely or inappropriately and there will be unscrupulous people who will take advantage of eighteen-year-olds who access their $54,000; 2) It would be a waste of government funds to create an infrastructure to police and prevent misuse of the Futures Funds.

I believe, but cannot yet prove, that the government's investing in education and an equity stake in society via homeownership will solidify the middle and the working classes and turn out to be a policy that can truly help individuals and the society at large. A program that offers a future to children—an education beyond high school and a chance to own a first home—is a program that will work. But it will take a decade before the full benefits of the Futures Account will be realized.

This lag between concept and reality may well be a good idea. An important feature of an effective social policy is that it does not offer a quick fix built on platitudes such as "children are a precious treasure." None of the three effective government programs described above—Social Security, the GI Bill, or Medicare—provided a quick fix. It was the investment, intended or not, in the future of the policies that produced their long-lasting success.

Chapter 6

ROUND UP THE USUAL SUSPECTS

There are a number of ways to prevent a new policy proposal from coming into existence. The first is to analyze and critique the proposal and identify all the flaws. Since there are no data on whether the new policy can be brought to scale and have a positive impact on a large population, critiquing any new large proposal is easy. A second approach is to hold fast to the existing policies and programs and argue that with more money or some minor changes, they would become far more effective. A third approach is to recognize and accept all the limitations of existing policies but argue that change would be even more disruptive and create more problems.

In 1996, I was working as a congressional fellow on the House Committee on Ways and Means. I was convinced that an existing government policy, the Adoption Assistance and Child Welfare Act of 1980 (Public Law 96-272), was not only ineffective, but was actually costing children's lives. I wrote a book making that argument, *The Book of David*,[1] and was working with a colleague, Cassie Bevan, to draft a new law that would prioritize child safety and well-being as opposed to family preservation. Another colleague, American Enterprise Institute scholar Douglas Besharov, warned me that my efforts might be counterproductive because, although the policies of Public Law 96-272 might be ineffective and harmful, the government and nonprofit agencies had already figured out how to subvert their most difficult parts. He pointed out that a change in policy, no matter how well intended, would create too much disruption.

The bottom line, as illustrated in the following allegorical story, is that in social policy, as in other areas of life, people are not simply resistant to change, they resist any change that impacts their own self-interest. This chapter is about how ineffective social policies remain in place and block new policies—a practice that I call, with a bow to the 1942 film *Casablanca*, "rounding up the usual suspects."

Fire the Watchman

Once there was a small widget company that, because of an unexpected increase in demand, found itself manufacturing widgets around the clock. So many widgets were being made that the company had to build a warehouse to store its products. When the company began to worry about some disaster befalling the warehouse full of widgets, one of the managers suggested that they hire a watchman to guard the widgets. And so they did.

As the inventory continued to grow, the managers became increasingly uneasy about having an unsupervised, minimum-wage employee guarding their valuable assets. So, at the suggestion of a manager, the company hired a supervisor for the watchman. Since the supervisor's job was to watch the watchman, the company built an office in the warehouse for the supervisor, bought furniture, and installed office equipment. To make sure the supervisor was doing his job, they also required him to submit monthly reports. Soon the supervisor complained that the time spent filing the reports was so great she could not properly supervise the watchman, and so the company hired a secretary for the supervisor. Business grew and eventually the managers realized they had so much to do, they did not have time to actually read the supervisor's reports. In addition, they were increasingly concerned that no one was watching the supervisor and the watchman and that together both could pilfer valuable widgets. The managers decided to hire someone to manage the supervisor and watchman.

The manager they hired had considerable experience in security and requested an office in the main building, a secretary, and an administrative assistant. While this seemed to be a big staff, the managers wanted the best person for the job, so they agreed to the requests and also gave their new manager the title of Vice President for Security. The new vice president was shocked to find lax performances by the supervisor, secretary, and watchman—he felt they didn't know the first thing about industrial security. Since he was busy meeting with the other vice presidents, he could not take time to provide the proper training, so he went out and hired a person to provide security training to the staff. And because he wanted a topflight trainer, he hired someone with considerable experience in industrial security. The new trainer soon requested her own secretary to prepare the training curriculum and schedule the training sessions. The director of training and the vice president for security and their staff realized they needed more space, and so they requested that the company build them a new suite of offices, which the company did.

Things went well for months, and the managers of the company, fearing that their vice president for security might leave for a better job, promoted him to Executive Vice President for Security and Company Affairs.

Sadly, as with so many manufacturing booms, the demand for widgets ended and the company found itself with too many widgets, too few customers, and a dwindling profit margin. Wanting to protect their profits and assure the stockholders that the company was doing everything it could to protect their investments, the managers decided they needed to cut costs. They couldn't throw out the widgets or tear down buildings, so the logical budget item to cut was personnel. They fired the watchman.

In case the story is too subtle, my point is to demonstrate that the bloated bureaucracy remained in place and the lowest person on the totem pole, the person who actually performed the necessary task of watching the warehouse, was let go.

THE MAKING OF AN ISSUE AND THE CREATION OF A GOVERNMENT AGENCY

Given how private troubles are transformed into social issues and finally social problems, there is rarely an existing government agency to address the newly identified social problem. Thus, an initial government response is to set up or build up an agency—much like expanding a widget company when demand increases.

Duties and responsibilities that were shared or incorporated into existing agencies are reallocated to a new division or agency. For example, the issue of child abuse and neglect was the responsibility of the United States Children's Bureau, which was a division within the then U.S. Department of Health, Education, and Welfare. The Children's Bureau had drawn public and professional attention to the problem of abuse and neglect and had developed and disseminated a model child abuse reporting legislation.[2] When Congress enacted the Child Abuse Prevention and Treatment Act of 1974, they created the National Center on Child Abuse and Neglect. This new agency was initially housed within the Children's Bureau, and at the beginning it was but a small office staffed by a person from that bureau. Over time, the office and the staff grew and the mandate and mission expanded—as did the definition of what constituted child maltreatment. The same process occurs with any other government legislation that addresses a new social welfare problem, including the Individuals with Disabilities Act, the Americans with Disabilities Act, the Violence Against Women Act, and the establishment of the Office of Homeland Security.

Step one is the creation of the responsible government agency. Step two is the institution of a funding stream. Legislation typically authorizes a funding level and then the actual funding must be appropriated by the legislature. On occasion, a legislator or the president can block spending for a problem he or she opposes. For example, in the 1980s Congress enacted a number of laws to provide federal oversight and funding for the prevention of domestic violence. The Reagan administration chose not to spend the money and thus never staffed the then Office of Domestic Violence. A fully funded and staffed Office of Domestic Violence did not come into being until the 1994 passage of the Violence Against Women Act.

Initial funding streams almost always exceed the capacity of the small neophyte government office's ability to spend the money. However, the inviolable rule of government is to spend your agency's allocation, and so in the start-up phase, spending patterns are often bizarre, if not outright irrational.

The Child Abuse Prevention and Treatment Act of 1974 set aside funding for research and demonstration projects. The Children's Bureau staff generated a call for proposals and evaluated the proposals. The problem was that few agencies or organizations were in a position to actually prepare proposals and submit them by the deadline. Thus, the funding far exceeded the number of proposals that met even a modest level of acceptability. Rather than fund unworthy proposals or, worse, not commit all the monies authorized and appropriated by Congress, the Children's Bureau grant managers came up with a novel resolution—they gave applicants more funding than they requested. One applicant, who had asked for $25,000 to start a child abuse treatment program, found that she had been awarded $250,000—and this was not an error, it was a conscious choice by the government program officer. I had my own grant funding doubled in the same funding cycle, so I know this was not a one-off event. Once the grantee realized the $250,000 award was not a mistake, she confronted the reality that she had no idea how to spend that much money. In the end, she spent so much time and effort looking for and hiring a staff, she never did get to implement the proposed treatment program.

What Happens When the Effectiveness of Government Programs Is Questioned

And so, the personal trouble becomes a social problem and a government program and agency are born. The program and agency reach out and attempt to address the problem. Some efforts are successful, or at least appear to be successful. Some are, at worst, benign, and have little positive or negative impact on the clients. And some efforts fail in a spectacular or tragic fashion. Whether the program seems to succeed, is more or less benign, or appears to be a train wreck, what happens when the government's effectiveness is questioned? In my experience, there is a consistent and systematic effort to "round up the usual suspects" to explain or justify why government failed to help.

Suspect Number 1: More Money

Money is the cure and the curse of social policy. A law or an agency cannot address social problems without money—this is obvious. When social problems are personal troubles, money determines the amount and quality of help brought to bear on solving the problem. I recall Dr. Ray Helfer, one of the pioneers in the study and treatment of child abuse, lecturing about the risk factors that can lead to abuse. Ray was a pediatrician and took a decidedly psychological approach to child abuse. By the early 1970s, he had developed his own version of a causal model and risk assessment device, which he labeled WAR—the World of Abnormal Rearing. His lecture outlined the personal and social factors involved in child maltreatment. To illustrate his point, he described what occurred in his own home with the birth of a new child. The changes produced significant stress, which he ameliorated by flying in his mother-in-law to help with the new baby. Clearly, in his case money could help deal with a personal trouble. But when money is not available, coping with stress becomes more difficult. In our economy, when money is not available to a large number of people, this is no longer a personal trouble, but a social problem. And government will inevitably be asked to provide the funds to deal with it.

Consider the scenario that unfolded in Hawaii with the Felix lawsuit. The problems created when Jennifer Felix was moved from Texas to Hawaii (over the objections of her family) were resolved because her family was able to pay for a service provider to fly from Texas to help develop an appropriate program for Jennifer. But for thousands of parents in Hawaii with special-needs children and limited funds, the money had to come from the state.

Once government is committed to helping, the money spigot opens slowly. In Hawaii, in the first year of implementing the consent decree, the total estimated funding for Felix-class services was $181 million. The class at this time consisted of 2,894 schoolchildren. This number increased somewhat geometrically for the next few years (up to 6,400 a year later, then 8,400, and finally nearly 12,000 in school year 1999–2000). Funding, on the other hand, initially increased arithmetically, up to $205 million a year after the consent decree, then down to $203 million a year later. But in 1998, with the deadline looming in twenty-four months, the state budget began its rapid increase. Funding increased from $230 million in 1998–1999 to $301 million a year later, and the request for the following year jumped another $100 million to $400 million.[3]

A second example of funding growth is the allocation of federal funds for child maltreatment. The majority of federal funding is provided under Title IV-E of the Social Security Act of 1935. The act contains the primary sources of federal funds available to states for child welfare, foster care, and adoption services. Title IV-E federal funding assists the states with providing out-of-home services for children (i.e. foster care), assistance in placing children in adoptive homes, and funding for children who age out of the foster care system. Title IV-E is an open-ended entitlement, which means the federal government will match state spending for qualified programs. In 1988, the total federal allocation for foster care services, as well as administration and training, was $1.1 billion. Funding nearly doubled in four years to $2.2 billion in 1992. Funding doubled again in four years to $4 billion in 1996. The expected allocation for 2011 was $4.5 billion.[4] The geometric increase in foster care funding has actually stopped.

Once residual programs are ramped up and running, the reality is *there really never is enough money.* When Congress enacted the Individuals with Educational Disabilities Act in 1973, the expectation was that the federal government would contribute 40 percent of the costs of the programs required under the law. But Congress never met this commitment, and the federal portion of special education costs was about 17 percent, or $3.7 billion in 1999–2000. With regard to child welfare, the initial estimate of 50,000 abused and neglected children gave way to the reality of millions of reports per year. The cost of conducting investigations sapped local budgets, which were also drained by the rising costs of out-of-home care. Even though Title IV-E is one of the few federal open-ended entitlements, the states still have to come up with their share of the costs of out-of-home care. With more than half a million children in out-of-home care on any given day, the state costs of foster care are enormous.

It's clear that regardless of the funding level of residual social welfare programs, it is never enough. When a crisis hits or when a program is criticized as ineffective, more money is believed to be the cure for all ills. Thus, the first suspect rounded up when government programs fall short of the mark is, "We need more money."

Suspect Number 2: More Staff

In the spring of 2002 the Florida Department of Children and Families was forced to admit that they had "lost" one of the children in their care. Five-year-old Rilya Wilson was a neglected child in Dade County, Florida. Her mother was alleged to be a drug addict and the Florida Department of Children and Families took Rilya into its care and placed her and her two siblings with their grandmother. Rilya's case became a national scandal when it was discovered in April 2002 that no one from the state had been in contact with Rilya for fifteen months. According to Rilya's grandmother, someone claiming to be a state caseworker removed Rilya from the home in January 2001!

Rilya had vanished and has never been seen since. For more than a year, no one from the Department of Children and Families noticed. Florida Circuit Judge Cindy Lederman lashed out at the agency, calling their actions "absolutely despicable."[5] Lederman's anger was fueled by the fact that Rilya's caseworker had told her in March 2001 that Rilya was in daycare. The caseworker submitted a report to Judge Lederman in August claiming that Rilya's custodian was addressing her needs. Not only did the caseworker misinform and deceive the judge, she also failed to enter any notes into Rilya's case file for fifteen months. Moreover, no supervisor was aware of either the deception or the lack of case notes.

The publicity around the lost girl generated the predictable anger from all concerned. The then Florida Department of Children and Families Secretary, Kathleen Kearney, said that Lederman had every right to be exceptionally angry. State Representative Sandra Murman said, "It doesn't take a very smart person to figure out something is very wrong there."[6]

The first suspect rounded up was the caseworker, followed by the creation of the inevitable blue-ribbon panel. The caseworker had already resigned a month before the revelations about the missing girl, but had she not resigned, she most certainly would have been fired. In June 2002, three department workers involved in Rilya's case were fired. The governor-appointed panel came back with usual suspect number one: they recommended that the state legislature appropriate money for substantial pay raises for DCF caseworkers and their supervisors, and provide funding for a Guardian ad Litem program, which provides attorneys or volunteers to represent children's interests in court proceedings. The panel avoided one of the usual suspects: a call for the department head's resignation.

It would be the national child advocates who would round up usual suspect number two—more staff. An article in *Child Protection Reports*, a newsletter widely read by child advocates, noted that, given Rilya's case, child advocates were wondering again just what it takes to get more resources pumped into child welfare services, "where in Florida and elsewhere, many feel services are woefully underfunded and stretched way beyond capacity."[7] The article went on to note that Rilya's case highlighted the all-too-familiar shortcomings of DCF—underfunded, understaffed, and stretched to the breaking point.

Newspapers in Florida, which had been unusually vigilant and critical of the Department of Children and Families, echoed the call for more staff. An editorial in *The Ledger* in Lakeland, Florida, stated: "As we've often noted, the DCF's basic problem is a lack of resources to carry out its mission. That means a shortage of caseworkers and investigators, and an inability to hire and keep qualified personnel. Only the Florida Legislature can solve that problem, and it's never shown any inclination to do so" (June 17, 2002, A-10).

The Rilya Wilson case provided an opportunity to echo the call for more staff that was heard in Florida four years earlier, when six-year-old Kayla McKean was killed by her father after DCF workers returned her to him. The same cry is heard nationally nearly every time there is a tragedy in the child welfare system: "Tragedies are the result of overworked, underpaid staff, and tragedies will only be prevented when staff are not overworked and underpaid." It is not only tragedies in child welfare systems that trigger the call for more staff. In virtually every residual social program, when the program falls short of the mark, when services are poor, when mistakes are made, a portion of the blame inevitably falls on the "overworked, underpaid staff." And while the staff members are indeed often overworked and underpaid, providing more staff does not resolve the fundamental problems.

Suspect Number 3: More Training

If the crisis is big enough, if the governor, mayor, or county officials feel vulnerable, and if there is not a major fiscal crisis, more money will be secured to hire more staff. The monies allocated and the staff positions authorized will almost always be less than was requested. Staff hired in a crisis tends to be frontline staff—as was the case with the widget company that hired the watchman first and the management personnel later. The new staff is likely to be young and inexperienced. I have noted many times that the typical frontline child welfare worker is a newly graduated college student who majored in art history or the humanities. Of course, sometimes the government falls below even minimum levels of qualification. In Hawaii, when a case aid was not available to work with an autistic child, the school bus monitor was pressed into service.

The new hires and many of the experienced staff often receive minimum training before they are given a full workload. In some jurisdictions child welfare workers are given only twenty hours of training before they are sent out to manage twenty to twenty-five families. In Hawaii's attempt to comply with the terms of the Felix consent decree, the departments of health and education were confronted with a workforce that had little if any training in autism, oppositional defiant disorder, and the other complex emotional and learning problems of children.

An inexperienced and youthful workforce facing complex social and psychological problems summons up the third usual suspect—"We need more training." In 2001, the Administration for Children's Services (ACS) in New York City was sued by women who claimed their constitutional rights were violated by ACS's practice of removing children from the homes where domestic violence occurred—even if the women were not offenders and had done nothing to harm their children. One of the solutions proposed by the plaintiffs was to provide ACS workers with more training on domestic violence. Similarly, the technical assistance panel formed by the court monitor in Hawaii provided numerous training sessions for educators, school administrators, and community mental health workers.

So what is wrong with more training? Isn't it better to have a young trained workforce than a young untrained workforce? Why diminish the value of training? The answer is that trainings often do not actually increase performance, accountability, or even knowledge. I myself conduct forty to fifty trainings each year, some lasting a half day, some lasting two or three days. I invest hours in developing my curricula, handouts, overheads, PowerPoint presentations, and the like. But the reality is that the basic training model consists of having people sit through sessions that are primarily didactic. There may be some exercises or small-group work, but the majority of trainings are delivered in the same talk-and-listen mode as elementary, secondary, and college education. The actual knowledge and skill gained from this mode of education is limited.

If the mode of the trainings is suspect, their actual content is often completely inadequate and inaccurate. The calls for training are not matched by calls for quality control. The plaintiffs in the class action suit in New York City wanted more training, but they presented only an untested curriculum that had been used in another city. In fact, the testimony of one of the plaintiff's witnesses contained a number of factual errors, including the claim that arresting domestic violence offenders significantly reduced the likelihood of future violence. In Hawaii, considerable monies were spent for training health department workers in a form of therapy that was unproven for the population it was meant to help. The trainees did not know that they were being trained in an approach that was entirely experimental; they were told the training was for a program that would be effective.

It is not that training is bad or useless; it is that the call for more training is not accompanied by calls for effective training of the trainers, careful quality control of the content and curriculum, and careful benchmarking and assessment of whether the trainings are producing better and more effective services and programs.

Suspect Number 4: Fire the Manager

When the Rilya Wilson case exploded into the headlines in Florida, it was the latest in a serious of crises faced by the then secretary of the Department of Children and Families. The secretary had been appointed by incoming governor Jeb Bush on the heels of the tragic death of Kayla McKean. The new secretary, Judge Kathleen Kearney, had built a reputation as a fierce child advocate while on the bench in Broward County, earning the nickname "the terminator" for her willingness to terminate abusive parents' parental rights. Kearney became even more controversial when she publicly criticized the staff of the department for their inability to keep children safe. She became the lightning rod for the agency she would lead, and soon enough she was the singular focus whenever there was a tragedy, error, or in the case of Rilya Wilson, an inexplicable blunder.

After a honeymoon period of about a year, during which Kearney positioned herself as an outsider come to reform the agency, she became an insider who was to blame for the agency's failings. By the time of the Rilya Wilson disappearance, the drumbeat for her resignation and the calls for the governor to replace her dominated the media coverage of her department.

Kearney escaped calls for her replacement in May 2002, but eventually resigned in July. Like many other social welfare administrators, she had about the same job security as the manager or coach of a professional sports team. When a forty-man football team, a twenty-five-man baseball team, or an eleven-woman basketball team falls into a losing streak, it is the coach or manager who is replaced, not the players.

On occasion, the change in leadership improves the team or even the agency. This happened in New York City in 1996. The embattled New York child welfare system suffered a major public scandal in 1995, when Eliza Izquierdo was killed by her mother after being returned home from foster care. Mayor Rudolph Giuliani's response was to eliminate the Child Welfare Agency and create the Administration for Children's Services. (Changing the agency's name is another "usual suspect" strategy. In Rhode Island, after a horrible child fatality, the then commissioner of the Department of Children and Families changed the agency's name to Department of Children, Youth and Families. When I asked her why, she replied, "The old agency name had a bad connotation among the public." I suggested that if she called it "Department of Nice People and Good Deeds" she would never have to change the name again.) In New York, Giuliani put former deputy mayor Nicholas Scoppetta at the helm as commissioner. Scoppetta himself had been a foster child, and during his six-year term as commissioner he helped settle a twenty-year-old class action lawsuit against the department and turn the agency around. There are effective leaders like Scoppetta, but, by and large, changing the chief administrator is about as successful as a baseball team replacing the manager—the same bad team remains and the losses continue.

Suspect Number 5: Form a Blue-Ribbon Panel

This suspect is so widely used and so transparent that its part in deflecting claims of government ineffectiveness is almost comical. When Rilya Wilson's disappearance was made public in Florida, Governor Jeb Bush's immediate response was to call together a blue-ribbon panel and give them ten days to prepare a report on the Department of Children and Families. The panel concluded that DCF failed to enforce its own protective measures and to enact other basic, commonsense policies. Yet the panel concluded that the people running DCF were not to blame and should not lose their jobs. Of course, the local media saw through this usual suspect and concluded, "What the governor touted as a 'blue-ribbon' panel was a whitewash panel."[8]

Even when a panel's qualifications and objectivity are impeccable, the end result is often a report presented at an emotion-packed press conference and then placed on a shelf next to the previous reports written, reported, and shelved. Only the most Pollyannaish optimists can believe that a blue-ribbon panel's report will have any meaningful impact on the actual functioning of social welfare agencies.

Suspect Number 6: Excuses, Excuses

The first five usual suspects are generally enough to fend off fallout from the occasional crisis or tragedy. But problems and shortcomings can be chronic, especially in larger agencies. And, in some situations, the four usual suspects have already been rounded up. Thus, there is a fallback set of excuses that become a mantra-like response to agency shortcomings.

a) He/she/they fell through the cracks. In the summer of 1994, four-year-old Amanda Froistad was living with her mother in Rapid City, South Dakota. Amanda's parents were divorced and the custody agreement called for Amanda to spend summers with her mother and the rest of the year with her father in Bowman, North Dakota. Amanda's aggressive behavior concerned her daycare providers. They told Amanda's mother, Ann Purdy, that Amanda should see a counselor because if her aggression toward the other children continued, she would not be allowed to remain in the daycare program. Ann took Amanda to a counselor and, during the very first session, Amanda indicated that her father was sexually molesting her.

The counselor, as was her legal responsibility, reported this allegation to the local office of the South Dakota Child Welfare Agency. The case was assigned for investigation, but the investigator believed she had no authority to proceed, as the alleged abuser—Amanda's father, Larry—lived in North Dakota. The investigator referred the case to Bowman County, North Dakota. There, caseworker Connie Klein consulted with her supervisors and was told she could not investigate the case because the child was out of the county's jurisdiction. No investigation was ever conducted in either state.

Amanda's mother attempted to have the custody order changed, but the judge in North Dakota refused to do so. Thus, Amanda returned to her father in Bowman, North Dakota, in December 1994. Even though Connie Klein knew Amanda was back with her father, she did not conduct an investigation, although she did arrange for a "courtesy interview" with Larry, which was held with Connie and the Bowman County sheriff. Nothing else was done. Over the next few months, neighbors and teachers expressed concern about Amanda. She was often not dressed properly for the cold weather, seemed unsupervised much of the time, and was wetting herself at school. They reported their concerns to Connie Klein, but no investigation was initiated. In May 1995, there was a fire at Larry and Amanda Froistad's home and Amanda perished. An investigator from the local fire department ruled the fire an accident, caused by an electrical problem. Amanda was buried and Larry moved to San Diego.

Three years latter, in March 1998, Larry Froistad confessed to setting the fire that killed his daughter. Some observers hypothesized that Larry killed Amanda to prevent her from revealing the abuse. Froistad's confession was made on an internet chat group. Apparently, someone in the chat group reported him to the FBI. Froistad was arrested, and when his computers were examined, investigators found photo and video evidence of his sexual molestation of his daughter.

Ann Purdy sued South Dakota and North Dakota child welfare administrators and caseworkers for the wrongful death of her daughter. Caseworkers in neither state had met their legal duties to conduct an investigation. Connie Klein did not respond to the concerns of neighbors and schoolteachers in Bowman. The training of the director of the Bowman County Social Service was woefully inadequate: it consisted of four years of high school and two years of cosmetology school.

How did officials respond when accused of nonfeasance that brought about the death of a five-year-old? They said Amanda "fell through the cracks." When Eliza Izquierdo was killed by her mother in New York City, officials of the child welfare agency said she "fell through the cracks." When Kayla McKean was killed by her father in Florida, the state's explanation for its lack of supervision of a child in its care was "she fell through the cracks."

One has to wonder (yes, this is a rhetorical question) just how many cracks there are and how big they are. In fact, these are not small cracks—many of them are the size of the Grand Canyon. Moreover, they are not randomly placed; they are structural fissures endemic to many social welfare programs.

*b) **Things are better now.*** The "he/she/they fell through the cracks" excuse deflects responsibility for nonfeasance, malfeasance, or ineptitude away from the agencies and their personnel. A second excuse is sometimes used to deflect attention away from the first one. In this case, the agency administrator accepts responsibility for past shortcomings but explains that "that was then, this is now." And things are better now.

During the time I was examining Hawaii's compliance with the Felix consent decree, I presented a number of interim reports to the superintendent of schools, the director of the Department of Health, and the office of the attorney general. Each agency executive's response was, "The report is out of date; things are better now." When I presented my findings to the joint committee of the legislature responsible for oversight of the Felix compliance efforts, the administrators again deflected my critical comments by saying, "Things are better now; we are close to compliance." Hawaii remained out of compliance until 2005 and questions are still being raised about whether the state is meeting its obligations to special-education children.

*c) **Kill the messenger.*** One tried-and-true excuse is simply to "kill the messenger." If a person, advocacy group, consultant, or report criticizes the government, a typical strategy is to impugn the critic. My report on the Felix compliance efforts, which I submitted to the legislative auditor of

Hawaii, immediately set off a coordinated attempt to kill the messenger. The agency heads charged that I had no expertise in special education—despite the fact that the team I had assembled had extensive expertise in disabilities and special education and included a board-certified child and adolescent psychiatrist whose specialty was disabilities.

The agency heads attempted to attack my integrity, but they discovered that actually I had not been compensated for conducting the study—I had accepted a grant to the School of Social Work that did not include any salary for me. One of the plaintiffs' attorneys, frustrated by my concerns about the possible conflict of interest of the court-appointed monitor, went on public radio and threatened to sue me for libel. When I responded that I was prepared to defend my report and myself, the attorney sunk to calling me a buffoon. This may have been one of the kindest criticisms I received during my investigation of the flaws and waste in the Felix case. Consultants and advocates who criticize government ineptitude are rarely praised for their efforts.

I was lucky. I lived five thousand miles away from Hawaii and the Felix case. The critics of the compliance efforts were not metaphorically killed, but they became, in their own words, "radioactive." Agencies that criticized the governor and the heads of the Department of Health and Department of Education no longer received contracts from health or education departments. Employees who criticized Felix-related actions were reassigned or terminated. The assistant attorney general who uncovered the first case of overbilling was reassigned shortly after the guilty plea was announced. Case managers who criticized procedures received no more cases, and so on. The Felix compliance effort was spending $400 million per year, and providers either quietly accepted Felix monies or found themselves "radioactive."

The messenger need not be an individual. In the 1980s, federal legislation created a national advisory committee on child abuse and neglect. The committee issued their first report in 1990. It was a stinging rebuke of federal and state efforts to prevent and treat child abuse:

> In spite of the nation's avowed aim of protecting children, each year *hundreds of thousands* of them are being starved and abandoned, burned or severely beaten, raped and sodomized, berated or belittled.

The report continued:

> [T]he *system* the nation has developed to respond to child abuse and neglect is *failing*. It is not a question of acute failure of a single element of the system; there is a chronic and critical multiple organ failure.[9] (emphasis in the original)

The advisory board went on to write two more reports; the second one, published in 1995, focused on child fatalities. The government's response to the reports was silence. Two more critical reports were issued—both were met with government silence. The Clinton administration chose not to appoint members to the advisory board after the 1995 report, and then, in 2002, Congress eliminated the legislative requirement even to have an advisory board.[10]

CONCLUSION

Rounding up the usual suspects does not fix what is broken. These suspects have been rounded up for decades and government social programs are still too often unable to help. The lesson is clear: the social service emperor has no clothes. A second lesson, which is a bit subtler, is that once government programs are established, it is extremely difficult to change them, irrespective of whether they help or harm. Proposing a new policy that requires confronting or eliminating existing and entrenched programs is a tactic that always encounters considerable resistance.

One possible means of moving toward new and better policy is by bringing research into the discussion. My efforts to bring about a change in child welfare law were greatly enhanced by both my research credentials and accomplishments and by the persistent presentation of research results that demonstrated the problems and unanticipated consequences of family preservation programs.

Chapter 7

THE DRUNK AND THE LAMPPOST

In an ideal world, scientific evidence would guide social policy. But this is not an ideal world and often no available evidence speaks to the effectiveness of a proposed program or even an existing one. In fact, high-quality research evidence is sometimes available, but it is ignored for one reason or another. Or there is evidence of program effectiveness but the program is applied outside the range or scope of the actual research findings—the pharmaceutical analogy would be taking a drug that effectively reduces high blood pressure and using it to treat acne. In the end, when it comes to applying research to social policy and programs, the world we live in is neither ideal nor simple.

One constraint to developing evidence-based social policy is the fact that policymakers have no particular interest in applying research. David Ford, a longtime scholar in the field of domestic violence, is fond of saying: "Research is to policymakers and practitioners what a lamppost is for a drunk—to be used more for support than illumination." Research should guide policy and practice, especially when it comes to establishing and maintaining social safety nets. There is nothing crueler than to purport to provide a safety net for those in dire need and then to offer up nothing more than a tissue of ideologies, profit-seeking marketing, or programs designed more to employ social service providers than to help those in need. And yet, as Ford so pointedly emphasizes, research is rarely the thread of social safety nets.

The late Senator Daniel Patrick Moynihan provided a perfect example of David Ford's point about research. Moynihan was chairman of the Senate Finance Committee in 1993, at the opening of the Clinton administration. The country then, as now, was in a recession, and Moynihan's committee was charged with producing $500 billion in deficit reduction—aka program cuts. In the face of this daunting budget-reduction task, Moynihan and his committee were lobbied by officials in the new administration to find new funding for favored social programs.

Among these was one Moynihan sarcastically referred to as his "favorite": family preservation. It was a favorite, not because Moynihan embraced the program or believed it would work, but because, in his words, it was "another categorical aid program—there were dozens already in place—which amounted to a dollop of social services and a press release for some subcommittee chairman."[1] The program's cost would be $930 million over five years.

Moynihan decided to write a letter to the economist Laura D'Andrea Tyson, who at the time was chair of the President's Council of Economic Advisers. Moynihan assured Tyson he supported the president's proposal, but having read a recent evaluation of family preservation programs in Illinois, he had reservations. The report had concluded that "solid proof that family preservation services can affect a state's overall placement rate is still lacking."[2]

Despite the fact that the chairman of the Senate Finance Committee had specifically asked for evidence of the program's effectiveness, and the Clinton administration had failed to provide it, the funding was included in the budget approved by the Finance Committee and ultimately the House and the Senate. Funding for family preservation programs—programs for which, even in 2011, there is no solid empirical evidence of effectiveness—was the only new funding for social programs in the budget passed in August, 1993. Each year since then, the president has requested, and Congress has appropriated, continued funding for family preservation.

Research neither guided nor illuminated federal policy and funding for family preservation programs. In the Felix case, research was rarely used, and when it was it provided little illumination. This chapter examines the complex relationship between research and government programs, looking at another instance of what could have been a triumph of evidence-based social policy, if high-quality research had not been used to illuminate the wrong path.

The Case of MST: How Research Can Illuminate the Wrong Path

By January 2000, time was running out for the state of Hawaii and its departments of education and health. The court-appointed monitor, Ivor Groves, had established benchmarks that would have to be met by June 2000 in order for Judge Ezra to rule that the state was in *substantial* compliance with the terms of the 1994 consent decree. With six months to go, the state had made progress but was woefully short of meeting the benchmarks. Nonetheless, the departments pushed ahead with their work. Assistant Attorney General Russell Suzuki, who had negotiated the terms of the consent decree on behalf of the state, claimed that by June the state would be in substantial compliance. Suzuki may or may not have believed his own cheerleading, but he knew that saying the glass was half empty could demoralize the staff, and this would decelerate rather than accelerate the state agencies' and the legislature's efforts toward compliance.

The legislature returned to session in January 2000, and one of their first tasks was to hear requests for supplemental funding from various state agencies. The House Finance Committee met on February 14th to consider requests for supplemental funding for Felix compliance efforts. The Department of Education was not requesting more funds, but the Health Department's Community and Adolescent Mental Health Division came forward with a request for $17.7 million.

To anyone familiar with the process by which legislative finance or ways and means committees vet requests for any form of funding, let alone mid-year supplemental funding, the February hearing was remarkably short and perfunctory. Only a handful of legislators attended. When the deputy director of the Department of Health, Anita Swanson, presented her testimony, she was not asked a single question. The legislators knew enough not to block any requests for Felix funding at this late date, for fear of being labeled "obstructionists" or "anti-child." Whatever the agencies wanted, they got.

One of the items included in the funding appropriation was $1.2 million to support the implementation of a program called MultiSystemic Therapy (MST). Coincidentally, MST is based on similar assumptions and models as the family preservation programs funded by Congress in 1993. The amount was relatively small compared to the $300 million that was budgeted for Felix compliance efforts in fiscal year 2000. Neither the program nor the amount requested elicited questions from the committee members who were in attendance. I attended the hearing and the request for MST did catch my eye. I began raising questions after the hearing.

My first question was about why continuation funds were requested for MST. Did this mean that the program was already in place? The answer was yes; the Department of Health had begun implementing MST in July 2000. Whose idea was the program? The answer was that Christina Donkervoet promoted MST. Donkervoet was the chief of the Community and Adolescent Mental Health Division of the Department of Health. Donkervoet, a graduate of the University of Rhode Island School of Nursing, had studied and worked with Scott Henggeler at the

University of South Carolina. Henggeler had developed and carefully evaluated MST. I wondered aloud why MST was so central to the Felix compliance efforts as to merit a mid-year supplemental appropriation. The answer to this question was found in the court-appointed monitor's benchmarks, as stipulated in a court order of August 2000. Benchmark number fifty called for the implementation of MultiSystemic Therapy for the children who were in the Felix class.

My queries and palpable skepticism about MST were brushed off. I was reminded that MST was an evidence-based, carefully evaluated, and respected intervention. I, of all people, should have endorsed the program. Of all the activities and programs rolled out by the Department of Health as part of compliance with the Felix consent decree, MST was the best tested and most proven. It went beyond the standard of "best practices"; there was actual scientific evidence that MST was, in fact, effective.

The use of MST in Hawaii was an example of research used for illumination, not just support. But the issue of evidenced-based practice and policy turned out to be much more complex than simply using the results of sound research to successfully meet the needs of those who need government help.

MST: A Brief History

MST's web page summarizes its history and applications:

> Multisystemic Therapy (MST) was developed in the late 1970s to address several limitations of existing mental health services for serious juvenile offenders. These limitations include minimal effectiveness, low accountability of service providers for outcomes, and high cost....
>
> MST is a pragmatic and goal-oriented treatment that specifically targets those factors in each youth's social network that are contributing to his or her antisocial behavior. Thus, MST interventions typically aim to improve caregiver discipline practices, enhance family affective relations, decrease youth association with deviant peers, increase youth association with prosocial peers, improve youth school or vocational performance, engage youth in prosocial recreational outlets, and develop an indigenous support network of extended family, neighbors, and friends to help caregivers achieve and maintain such changes. Specific treatment techniques used to facilitate these gains are integrated from those therapies that have the most empirical support, including cognitive behavioral, behavioral, and the pragmatic family therapies.
>
> MST services are delivered in the natural environment (e.g., home, school, community).... The strongest and most consistent support for the effectiveness of MST comes from controlled studies that focused on

violent and chronic juvenile offenders. Importantly, results from these studies showed that MST outcomes were similar for youths across the adolescent age range (i.e., 12–17 years), for males and females, and for African-American vs. white youths and families.[3]

Not only does MST have a solid theoretical underpinning, the intervention has been rigorously evaluated since 1986. By 2000, the year in which the Hawaii Department of Health launched its MST initiative, the program had demonstrated successful outcomes in four randomized clinical trials with more than three hundred serious, violent, or substance-abusing juveniles and their families.

Randomized clinical trials, in which the subjects are randomly assigned to the experimental group (in this case MST) or a control group, are considered the "gold standard" for evaluating interventions or programs. The complexity of human behavior and the way social programs are implemented often preclude the use of a randomized clinical trial for evaluation. Thus, even one randomized trial would be rare; four are exceptional. Even more exceptional, the juveniles who went through the MST program showed reduced criminal activity, including drug abuse. In other words, MST was more effective than other methods or interventions that had been used to prevent continued juvenile delinquency. Finally, the positive results were achieved in a cost-effective fashion. In 1996 dollars, MST cost $4,000 per family. The average cost of a Felix-class child in 2000 was $25,500.

The Hawaii Implementation

Hawaii's Child and Adolescent Mental Health Division had firsthand knowledge of MST and an understanding of both the theory and the evidence supporting the program. And so the office set about to provide MST services to Felix-class children. Two different sub-populations were initially provided the treatment. The first group consisted of adolescents who were classified as "conduct disordered" as part of their Individual Education Plan (IEP). A second population, children with "emergent mental health disorders," also received MST. The two subpopulations were not a minority of the Felix-class children. Christine Donkervoet stated at one legislative hearing that more than half of the Felix-class children were classified as "conduct disordered."

Deconstructing the "Evidence"

On the surface, the Hawaii implementation of MST should have been a template for offering an evidence-based safety net to troubled youth. The intervention was founded on a solid theoretical base, and its effectiveness had been borne out by the highest quality evaluations. Moreover, there had been multiple evaluations, each of which supported the effectiveness of MST. Why would I question such a successful and cost-effective program?

I had four concerns about the use of MST in Hawaii. First, and by far the most important, was that although MST is an evidence-based program, it did not seem to me so critical as to be a benchmark for the state's compliance with the Felix case settlement. Second, the application of MST in Hawaii was going to extend the program to a population that had not been evaluated yet in the random clinical trials: juvenile sex offenders. This application was exploratory and experimental and, again, did not seem to justify establishing MST as a benchmark for compliance with the settlement. Third, while the program outcomes of MST are impressive—reduction in rates of rearrest, reduction in out-of-home placements, improvement in family functioning, and decreased mental health problems for serious juvenile offenders—the impact of MST on school performance is unknown. Fourth, I suspected that the requirement of using MST to comply with the Felix settlement was in part a job-creation program, since the person heading Hawaii's MST program was the husband of Christina Donkervoet, who, as mentioned above, was the chief of the Community and Adolescent Mental Health Division of the Department of Health.

There is a final caution, which goes to the heart of the complexity of evidence-based practice and policy: *the tendency to turn scientifically validated interventions into a one-size-fits-all policy*. The widespread application of family preservation programs lacked any scientific support. The scientific support for MST was strong; but was it strong enough to warrant it becoming a benchmark for Hawaii's compliance with the Felix settlement?

The Canadian Implementation and Evaluation of MST

Another evaluation of MST, this one conducted by a team of researchers in Canada, offers a valuable cautionary lesson about research "evidence" and the application of research to social programs and policy. Canada, too, has a significant problem with juvenile crime and juvenile delinquency. In the 1990s, the Ministry of Community and Social Services of Ontario was looking for a cost-effective means of reducing youth crime. By the end of the decade, word of the success of MST had spread at professional meetings and through scholarly publication channels. Ontario, like Hawaii, saw MST as an evidence-based and cost-effective means of reducing the direct costs of youth crime and the costs associated with criminal justice processing. Ontario, however, took a different approach from Hawaii in implementing MST.

Rather than accepting at face value the positive claims, Ontario chose to determine first whether the successes in the United States *could be replicated* in Canada. Canada's National Crime Prevention Centre supported an evaluation of MST in four southern Ontario communities—London, Mississauga, Simcoe County, and Ottawa. The Canadian evaluation was to be the same gold-standard randomized clinical trial that had been used to evaluate MST in the United States. About two hundred families in the four communities would receive MST between 1997 and 2001. At the same time, two hundred families would continue with the usual services that were available through the local youth justice services. The "usual" services consisted of probation supervision supplemented, as needed, with specialized therapeutic programs.

The families were followed to see if MST produced better outcomes for juvenile offenders than incarceration or probation. The key question was, again: "Would MST children have lower rates of juvenile crime than youth in the comparison group?" A second goal, modeled on the research in the United States, was to determine if the cost of MST—which was greater than that of the usual community services—was justified by the costs saved by not having to jail youth offenders.

By 2002, data had been collected and the interim results published.[4] The main outcome, unlike research findings from the United States, was that there were no distinguishable differences on any of the outcome measures. In other words, MST made no difference when used in Canada. Three years after the experiment began, nearly eight in ten of the youth had been convicted of another crime. In the United States, the rearrest rates were 25 to 70 percent lower for the juveniles whose families received MST.

The Canadian research team went beyond concluding that they could not replicate the positive outcomes achieved by MST in the United States. They finished their report with a section entitled "10 Ways to Come to the Wrong Conclusion." *This should be required reading for any policymaker, advocate, or agency administrator involved in decisions about safety-net social programs.* I have opted to modify their section headings to convey a more specific set of cautions about using research to support social policy.

a) Do not assume the results from one site will generalize to other communities, states, or nations. While twenty-three American states (including Hawaii) and several European countries have implemented or are implementing MST, the Canadians did not assume that results from South Carolina or other U.S. locations would apply to Canadian youth. Internationally, there has always been a tendency to think that innovative programs developed in the United States would be appropriate for other nations. Within the United States, well-described innovative programs that are consistent with the liberal values of service providers are quickly and widely implemented based only on a claim of effectiveness. But even high-quality scientific evidence is not sufficient proof that the intervention will be effective in other nations, societies, or cultures.

b) Do not assume improvements are due to the treatment. Most evaluations of social interventions or social programs are not random clinical trials. Most evaluations are either a "pretest/posttest only" design with no comparison group, or a "pretest/posttest" design with experimental and control groups that have not been created by random assignment. If the Canadian research team had used the typical pretest/posttest design, they would have measured the juveniles' attitudes and behaviors prior to the experimental intervention (MST). When the experiment or treatment was complete, they would again measure attitudes and behaviors. A pretest/posttest design is a common way to assess the impact of programs. Such a design, however, fails to determine whether the changes are due to the treatment or some other factors. When the Canadian research team compared the pretest and posttest scores of the youth who were provided MST, they found improvements in both attitudes and behavior. However, when the scores were compared to the randomly assigned control group, there were no differences between the groups in terms of improvements. In other words, both groups improved, but the change was not due to the MST intervention. When programs are tested using designs other than random clinical trials, there is the likelihood that change may be incorrectly attributed to the treatment.

c) Do not assume that improvements will translate into actual behavior. Many evaluations use psychological or attitude tests to assess whether the program was effective. One can change attitudes or psychological test scores without actually changing behavior. While in the Canadian study the MST children's psychological test scores improved, their actual behavior was no different from that of the control group— both had high rates of conviction for juvenile crimes. In the U.S. studies, the actual behavior did improve and there was less criminal activity after the MST intervention.

d) Do not generalize from a one-group design.   In the 1970s the United States was in the midst of what was called a "foster care crisis." More than 500,000 children were in foster care on any given day. The costs were enormous, and because so few children were successfully reunited with their families, the foster care population continued to rise. In the state of Washington, two clinicians developed a program they called "Homebuilders," which eventually evolved into "Family Preservation." The program's goal was to provide intensive services to families in crisis. The service providers would have small caseloads and would be available seven days a week, at all hours.

The initial results of the evaluations of Homebuilders and the more generic Intensive Family Preservation Services were quite promising. The most important outcomes were that fewer children needed to be placed outside of the home; those who were placed were able to return home more quickly; the costs of the program were reasonable; and the children seemed to be safe. These results were based on what researchers call "one-group design." Such a design can be a "pretest/posttest only" design, where the key variables are measured prior to and after the intervention, or it can be a "posttest only" design, where the key variable is measured only after the intervention. The "one-group design" is at the opposite end of the methodology continuum from the randomized clinical trial experiment—it is considered the weakest form of research design. Simply stated, one can claim wonderful outcomes for those receiving the intervention or services, but the question is: compared to whom? Unless one can compare those who receive the service to a control group—preferably one created through a randomized procedure—no actual conclusions can be reached. Not surprisingly, when random clinical trials of Homebuilders and Intensive Family Preservation Services were carried out, there were no indications of reduced placement, better child outcomes, or increased child safety.[5]

e) No matter what research design is used, do not base conclusions on evaluating only those individuals who complete a program.   Chances are, individuals or families who complete a program are more motivated to change their behavior, compared to those who drop out or never show up for the first appointment. One can easily support the effectiveness of a program by only assessing those who finish the program. To understand whether a program is effective, even when conducting a random clinical trial, all those who entered the program must be compared to the control group.

f) Do not base conclusions on the use of a single indicator of outcome. In the evaluation of the Intensive Family Preservation Services, the goal was to reduce placement, and so the outcome selected for assessment was placement. If placements were reduced, the program would be considered successful. However, and rather obviously, if reducing placements increased injury to children or increased child abuse fatalities, reducing placement could hardly be considered a successful intervention. The single indicator of outcome in the assessment of intensive family intervention was the wrong one, or should have been one of many outcomes measured, including child safety and well-being, risk of further injury, and family functioning.

g) Do not base conclusions and generalizations on a study that employs a small sample. My research colleagues find this an odd caution, since researchers know that small samples make it difficult to find statistically significant results. In Ontario, however, if the researchers had compared the results of only the first fifty families enrolled in the experiment, they would have concluded that the usual services were actually more effective than MST. It was only after analyzing the full results that the data showed no effect of MST. What happened? Well, it might be that in the early days of a new program, the service providers had greater difficulty using the new approach. On the other hand, if MST had been shown to be better, it might be that in the roll-out phase, the workers worked harder at delivering the service. Most likely, however, is that small samples are more affected by random fluctuations. One can flip a coin ten times and get six heads and four tails and assume the coin is not fair. After a thousand flips, the random fluctuations smooth out and the result is about fifty-fifty heads and tails. Thus, the larger the number of cases, the less likelihood that chance will influence the results.

h) Use a short follow-up. Perhaps the easiest way to come to the wrong conclusion about a program or intervention designed to prevent problems like delinquency, child abuse, or domestic violence is to use a short follow-up period. Short follow-ups can lead to the wrong conclusion, especially if the program is designed to prevent a rare event. Partners who abuse one another, adolescents who engage in delinquent behaviors, and even parents who physically or sexually abuse their children do not do so every day. In fact, on average, such behaviors may occur three or four times a year. If the follow-up evaluation period is six months, the behavior may not occur in this time frame, irrespective of the intervention. On the other hand, programs or interventions that are designed to produce positive or pro-social behavior may make a temporary difference that does not last over time. For example, a multi-million-dollar welfare-to-work program in Philadelphia was able to move welfare recipients into the workforce in a short period of time. However, after eighteen months, only 20 percent of the former welfare recipients were still employed. They had not been laid off, but had lost their jobs because of fighting at work, leaving the job without notifying a supervisor, or failing to notify an absence.

i) Study the program only in one place.   In the mid-1980s a research team in Minneapolis published the results of an experiment designed to see if arresting domestic violence offenders would reduce intimate partner assault. The study was a landmark project, because the research team was able to get permission from the chief of police in Minneapolis to implement a gold-standard random-trial field experiment.[6] In cases of misdemeanor-level domestic violence, a random procedure instructed the police to make one of three choices: arrest the perpetrator, separate the perpetrator from the victim, or offer advice and counseling. After six months (note the short follow-up), the researchers found that the men who were arrested were half as likely to reassault their partners as the men in the separation or mediation groups. Within weeks of the announcement of these findings, numerous police departments had implemented mandatory arrest. A few years after the publication of the results, the U.S. Department of Justice, National Institute of Justice funded five replications of the Minneapolis police experiment to find out if those results could be replicated in other cities. The replications were also designed to resolve some of the methodological problems that occurred in the Minneapolis study.

None of the studies could replicate the original Minneapolis findings. In some cities, Milwaukee for instance, arresting men who were employed and married did reduce their use of violence. But, more important, arresting men who were not married to their partners and who were unemployed increased the risk of violence. In Charlotte, Miami, Colorado Springs, and Omaha, arrest alone made no difference.

The lead researcher in the original Minneapolis study tempered his early enthusiasm for mandatory arrest after the publication of the replication studies.[7] The domestic violence field learned the hard way what Canada learned the easy way: just because a program appears to work in one place does not assure that it will work in all, most, or even any place else. Had the Canadians only assessed MST in one location, they might have come to the wrong conclusion. But they carried out the study in four sites and found no compelling evidence of the effectiveness of MST. Moreover, they learned that the ability of MST to reduce criminal behavior might depend on the characteristics of the youth referred, the nature of the communities' "usual services," and the many other complex factors related to program intervention. Similarly, because mandatory arrest for domestic abuse was assessed in multiple locations, the researchers learned that an offender's "stake in conformity"—for example, whether or not he is employed and risks losing the job in case of arrest—might influence whether the arrest will reduce violence or inflame it.

j) Use only one study.   This is a natural follow-up to the previous item. When it comes to social service programs, one or even a couple of studies are not enough to conclude that a program is effective or not. Confidence that a program is effective can only be built by examining the results of successive tests and evaluations.

Can You Lie with Statistics?

I have come to despise the book *How to Lie with Statistics*.[8] Darrell Huff's slim 1954 volume is not a bad book; in fact it is terrific. It shows how statistics and data presentation can be manipulated to bias conclusions. Among the more obvious ways to lie with statistics is to use samples that have a "built-in bias." Let's say, for example, I want to find out the average salaries of people who receive their MSW degrees from the University of Pennsylvania School of Social Policy & Practice. I ask my alumni office to contact a representative sample of our 2005 graduates. The results come back and, much to my surprise, the average (mean) salary is $65,000. Not bad for social workers. Of course, I did not bother to explain that we only sampled graduates for whom we had addresses. I also did not report on the number or percentage of graduates who failed to respond to the survey (usually about 50 percent). What I really learned was that those graduates we located and who chose to respond had an average salary of $65,000. It would not be accurate to say the average salary of one of our graduates is $65,000.

Huff also explains how "averages" can be gamed. In the statement about average salaries, I noted that this was the "mean" salary. As anyone who understands basic statistics knows, the mean is always affected by extreme scores. If a number of respondents are unemployed and report an income of zero dollars, this will pull the mean down. If one of our graduates decides to become a hedge fund manager, this could, depending on the year, drastically increase or decrease the mean. If I want to avoid the biases of extreme scores, I would report the "median" income—the amount above and below which half the graduates earned. Huff's little book provides more examples of lying with tables and figures, post-hoc analysis, and just bad math.

The reason I despise the book is that whenever I am in a discussion about program effectiveness, regardless of whether I am supporting or critiquing a program or policy, someone will cite the book *How to Lie with Statistics* as if the title alone was sufficient to undermine any and all arguments. Those who publicly cite the book may or may not have read it (I suspect there are more of the latter), but they use it as a sledgehammer to destroy any argument about program effectiveness with which they do not agree. The implicit logic of citing the book is that since anyone can lie with statistics, all research is suspect, and thus anecdotes, single cases, or personal and political values are just as viable and accurate as research in selecting social policies and programs.

And so, as a transition to the next section, I offer the following rebuttal: *just because one can lie with statistics does not negate the fact that there are rules of evidence in social science research that can be applied to evaluation research.* Rules of evidence are lie detectors or truth serums. They allow policymakers and program managers to weed out false and even outrageous claims and actually use research for illumination.

Rules of Evidence / Rules for Illumination

To say that there are rules of evidence is not to claim that social science or well-constructed evaluations can precisely and completely explain or predict human behavior. Social behavior is complex, and improvement in the human condition is not accomplished by simply matching a service to a condition. Before I get to the rules, let me begin with the caveats. First, as I emphasized earlier, *data is not the plural of anecdote.* No matter how compelling stories about a program or policy are, they are not the equivalent of social science data. Now I am quite aware of the irony of claiming that data is not the plural of anecdote in a book full of anecdotes. When I use anecdotes or stories I always have in mind that there should be quality actual data to support my argument. Nonetheless, I know how vulnerable I am to hoisting myself on my own principle.

Similarly, slick marketing or the imprimatur of a major foundation or corporation is not the same as good data. A few years ago Bill Moyers presented a public television special sponsored by the Edna McConnell Clark Foundation, one of the nation's best endowed and most proactive philanthropic organizations. The program focused on the effectiveness of the Homebuilders or Intensive Family Preservation Services. Moyers, PBS, and the Clark Foundation were a trinity of impressive credentials. That notwithstanding, at the time of the special there was not a single study complying with the normal standards for evaluation research that demonstrated the effectiveness of Homebuilders. Moyers, Oprah, Dr. Phil, Katie Couric, and their producers, sponsors, and networks do not individually or collectively constitute the rules of evidence. One must consider at least the following five rules before drawing conclusions about the effectiveness of any social policy program.

1. The Randomized Trial is the Gold Standard for Evaluating a Program.

It is impossible to overemphasize this rule. This is the standard the Food and Drug Administration uses to determine which drugs are effective and safe. This is the only method that can effectively rule out threats to the validity of conclusions about the effectiveness or ineffectiveness of programs, treatments, or policies.

2. Look at the Effect Size.

A randomized trial experiment may find statistically significant results—in other words, the treatment had an effect—but the strength of that effect is only determined by examining its actual size. During the summer of 2002, the prestigious *Journal of the American Medical Association* published the results of a major study on hormone replacement therapy.[9] This randomized trial study followed 16,608 women, half of whom took the combination of estrogen and progestin. The control group took a placebo. The experimental group and the control group were followed for an average of 5.2 years.[10]

The published results of the study stated that for every 10,000 women taking estrogen plus progestin pills (only tablets were used in the study):

- 38 developed breast cancer each year compared to 30 breast cancers for every 10,000 women taking placebo pills.
- 37 had a heart attack compared to 30 out of every 10,000 women taking placebo pills.
- 29 had a stroke each year, compared to 21 out of every 10,000 women taking placebo pills.

- 34 had blood clots in the lungs or legs, compared to 16 women out of every 10,000 women taking placebo pills.

There were some positive effects of progestin. For every 10,000 women taking estrogen plus progestin:

- 10 had a hip fracture each year, compared to 15 out of every 10,000 women taking placebo pills.
- 10 developed colon cancer each year, compared to 16 out of every 10,000 women taking placebo pills.

Within days of the release of these results, gynecologists were quoted in the newspaper and television recommending that women stop taking the combination of estrogen and progestin, and many postmenopausal women stopped taking it. For many women who stopped taking the drugs, the results must have been aversive—the return of hot flashes and difficulty sleeping. With the onset of the adverse symptoms, postmenopausal women anguished over whether to return to the drug and run the stated risk of cancer and heart disease, or to suffer through the hot flashes and other menopausal symptoms.

What the media and the women themselves overlooked was that although there were statistically significant harmful (and positive) outcomes, the actual size of the difference was small. In real numbers, it was a difference of seven women in the study. In probability terms the increased statistical risk was tiny.

3. Look under the Hood of the Sample.

Whether the research is a survey or a gold-standard experiment, the nature of the sample—how it was selected and whether it is representative—is key to the generalizability of the study results. While representative samples are an obvious requirement for any survey from which one wants to make generalizations, sampling techniques for experimental designs are often overlooked—at the peril of error. The sample should be appropriate not only in terms of generalization, but also in terms of the suitability of the sample for the intervention. It would be pointless to test MST or family preservation on a sample of college students.

Just as the representativeness of the sample is important, so too is the response rate. For surveys, the response rate is the percentage of those chosen to participate in the study who complete the survey. But for experiments that test the effectiveness of an intervention, the response rate is the percentage of those selected for inclusion in the study who actually enroll and complete the experiment. Gold-standard experiment results are compromised if the sample is creamed or skimmed from a population and represents only those motivated to engage in the treatment. In such a study, one would learn whether the treatment or intervention works for those motivated to change only. Nothing would be learned about resistant or reluctant participants.

4. Is the Measure and Measurement Appropriate?

In examining the results of family preservation efforts, Senator Moynihan noted that these programs did not reduce the number of children placed in foster care. He never actually questioned whether placement into foster care was the proper outcome measure to determine the effectiveness of the program. But the sociologist Peter Rossi, who also examined the effectiveness of family preservation, noted that "placement avoidance" was the wrong factor to be measured.[11] Rossi argued that placement avoidance was the intervention itself, not its result. If one wanted to know whether the program worked, the key variable that should have been measured was child well-being.

5. Fidelity.

The next rule of evidence is to determine whether the intervention delivery has high fidelity to the intervention model itself—that is, it is faithful to the design of the model. When the evaluations of family preservation programs found no effect, proponents claimed that the family preservation programs that had been evaluated were not faithful to, or had "high fidelity" with, the actual model of Homebuilders. This was indeed an appropriate response. Second- and third-generation implementations of social programs often water down the dosage of the intervention.

David Olds found this to be a problem with the evaluations of his "nurse home health visitor" programs designed to prevent child maltreatment. When Olds evaluated the program that used nurses, he found consistent and lasting positive results in terms of reduced child maltreatment.[12] However, when the intervention was provided by a layperson or paraprofessional, the program was not effective. Thus, in advocating for his program, Olds had to advocate for fidelity with the entire model, not just the concept of home health visiting.

One of the inhibitors that prevent government programs from working is diluting the program after research indicates the program is effective. Many state and county government agencies and budget offices cannot bear to pass up the opportunity to squeeze out additional cost saving, even at the expense of rendering a program ineffective.

THE LIGHT ON THE LAMPPOST

Policy by anecdote is the worst kind of social policy. Since I do not believe that bad research is better than no research, I have no regard for applying bad research—research that fails to meet the minimum standards of evidence—to social policy. But what about good research?

Using evidence to guide policy is not as simple as turning on the light on the lamppost and assuming it will illuminate. Perhaps the greatest danger posed by a move to evidence-based social policy would be to assume that a program, policy, or intervention that is supported by high-quality research should become the one-size-fits-all intervention. The Felix efforts in Hawaii took a perfectly good intervention, MST, and corrupted it by making it a mandate for compliance. When applying evidence to policy and practice, along with the guidelines and caveats I have reviewed in this chapter, it is essential to ask the question: "What works, for whom, and under what conditions?"

Chapter 8

THE EMPEROR'S WARDROBE CONSULTANT

In my nearly forty-year academic career, my goal has been to find ways to protect the safety and well-being of children. I have worked with child protective service agencies in the hope that what I have learned from my research will help provide those protections. My efforts have had their ups and downs, depending mostly on who was the secretary or commissioner of the state or local child protection system.

By 2006, my relationship with the Philadelphia Department of Human Services (DHS), the city agency responsible for child protective services, had reached an all-time low. My colleagues and I at the University of Pennsylvania, School of Social Policy & Practice, had completed a project aimed at improving the quality of the response to reports of suspected child abuse and neglect. As is often true, this initiative was sparked by public outrage about the death of a child who was supposed to be under the protection of the department. In this case, a baby had been killed by a caregiver after DHS received a report of suspected abuse. The caseworker claimed he had tried to visit the home, but the commissioner believed there had been no attempt to visit and that the caseworker had lied.

By the time we finished our examination of the department's procedures for investigating reported abuse and neglect, the commissioner who hired us had moved on to another position, and the new commissioner had no interest in our observations and recommendations. Adding insult to injury, the commissioner refused to pay for the work we had done, which included designing an entirely new process for investigating reports of suspected child abuse. Even though we had submitted the required reports, the new commissioner and her deputy simply stonewalled us. Their refusal to compensate us for our work was unprecedented. I knew that the university legal team would eventually succeed in getting us paid, but needless to say, the entire experience left me with a sour taste in my mouth (and a hole in our school's budget).

My mood deteriorated further when I became involved in two more cases of children who were supposed to be protected by DHS. In the first, I was hired as an expert witness to examine case files of a young girl who had been moved from foster care to the home of her half-sister's father. DHS had not required the father to undergo a medical examination, as would be required of any foster care provider; in fact, he should have been considered a foster care provider, since he was not the girl's biological father. It turned out the man was HIV positive. He sexually assaulted the little girl and when the abuse was uncovered, the girl was immediately moved to a new foster home. The agency failed to conduct a medical examination of the girl and failed to tell her new foster parent that the girl had been sexually assaulted by someone who was HIV positive. (The medical examination of the man was carried out after the assault.) The suit was brought by the foster mother when a medical examination revealed the girl was HIV positive. By this time the foster mother had adopted the girl. After I submitted my expert report, the city settled with the mother on behalf of the girl for $5.3 million.

The second case was more egregious. In the summer of 2006 I learned of the death of a fourteen-year-old girl with cerebral palsy, who had been a client of one of our MSW students. The student was about to be questioned by the Federal Bureau of Investigation. The FBI's involvement was surprising, since such child fatalities are local, not federal matters. But I learned that the FBI became involved because they suspected the agency where my student was placed had been misappropriating federal funds.

The misappropriation of funds was the least of the issues. The fourteen-year-old girl, Danieal Kelly, had starved to death. Over the course of months, she had wasted away to forty-two pounds. She died in a urine-soaked bed in a hot dark room, and when her body was discovered it was covered with bedsores and maggots. The case was supposed to be managed by a DHS contract agency—the agency at which our student was placed for his field practicum. DHS had received numerous reports of suspected maltreatment and had assigned an investigator to determine whether Danieal was being maltreated. At least two caseworkers from the contract agency and three caseworkers from DHS were supposed to be providing services to Danieal and her family and were required to be making regular home visits. Clearly, none of these obligations had been carried out.

Danieal's mother was convicted of manslaughter; she is serving a twenty- to forty-year sentence. The head of the contract agency went to prison for fraud. Six other employees of the contract agency were convicted of charges ranging from perjury to fraud. One DHS caseworker pled guilty to endangering a child, and a number of caseworkers and administrators were suspended or fired. At present (July 2011), another caseworker, Danieal's father, and the head of the contract agency are on trial. I knew the facts of this case long before the story appeared in the press. I had been asked by the Office of the District Attorney to testify before a grand jury regarding the numerous failings of DHS and the contract agency in the Kelly case.

These three cases roiled my rage. I simmered when the DHS commissioner ignored my recommendations about abuse reporting and refused to pay for the work our team had done. I boiled over when I learned about the HIV case and the death of Danieal Kelly. And then the media entered the picture.

Ken Dilanian and John Sullivan, reporters at the *Philadelphia Inquirer,* called me regarding their investigation of the DHS and child protective services in Philadelphia. Neither reporter had information about the HIV case or about Danieal Kelly. I could discuss the former with the reporters, since settlements involving public money are public information. There were some facts about the Kelly case I could share, because I had learned of them independent of my grand jury testimony. Other information came from my ongoing analysis of data on child abuse and foster care.

Dilanian and Sullivan interviewed me at length and checked and cross-checked facts. They also interviewed advocates and agency administrators. Their fact gathering went on for a few months. Their series would be published over five days, and they were exceptionally careful in preparing it.

At some point, Dilanian or Sullivan shared my comments with the commissioner of DHS. I knew this because a colleague who was conducting research was told DHS would block access to data if he had anything negative to say about DHS. He was led to believe that data access would be blocked if I continued to criticize DHS in my conversations with the press. My colleagues and codirectors at the University of Pennsylvania cautioned me that I would do great damage to our university and our efforts at system reform if I continued to talk to Dilanian and Sullivan. They cautioned me to tone down my comments if I couldn't manage to shut up altogether.

I considered my colleagues' cautions and the possible negative consequences to Penn researchers. I knew they were dependent on DHS cooperation for access to critical research data. Despite this, I decided to continue talking to Dilanian and Sullivan. I feel strongly that it is important to draw public attention to public systems' failures to protect children. The failures are outrageous and the public attention can lead to positive changes. The first segment of the series appeared on the front page of the *Philadelphia Inquirer* on Sunday, October 15, 2006. The headline, "Bury Your Mistakes," came from my quote: "In Philadelphia, you can bury your mistakes." The first segment discussed the fact that between January 2003 and October 2006, at least twenty-five children had died after the Philadelphia DHS had opened an investigation into possible abuse or neglect in the family. Neither the HIV case nor the Kelly case was mentioned in the first segment. When the story broke, my colleagues were convinced I had made a serious mistake and that our relationship with DHS and city government was irreversibly shattered.

The first installment prompted the mayor to discover for himself whether DHS was as troubled an agency as the newspaper article claimed. By Friday, Mayor John Street had learned about the Kelly case, and he wasted no time asking DHS Commissioner Cheryl Ransom-Garner to resign, firing Deputy Commissioner John McGee, and appointing an acting commissioner.[1]

DHS caseworkers protested in the streets in support of Ransom-Garner and McGee, and the mayor rounded up a "usual suspect" (see Chapter 6 on "blue ribbon commissions" as usual suspects), and appointed an oversight board to investigate DHS. The mayor's oversight board included five national experts. My colleagues and codirectors of Penn's Field Center for Children's Policy, Practice and Research, Carol Spigner and Cindy Christian, were appointed to the board. I knew and respected their abilities and that of the other three members.

Bringing public attention to the problem had positive results. Since the Dilanian and Sullivan series, the City of Philadelphia has elected a new major who hired a new commissioner for the Department of Human Services. By March 2011 the Mayor's Community Oversight Board issued a report outlining the many improvements that had occurred at the Department of Human Services.

When the oversight board (eventually titled the community review board) was formed, and each time the membership has changed, including in March 2011, I was and am still asked why I wasn't invited to serve on the board. After all, I have forty years of experience, am dean of a school, and was frequently quoted in Dilanian and Sullivan's series and in many follow-up articles. My response is always the same: *When you are the one who insists that the emperor has no clothes and is in fact naked, you are not going to be asked to be the emperor's wardrobe consultant.*

A POLICY CROSSROADS

I have spent my entire career pointing out when the emperor has no clothes, and I am not about to stop now. I devoted seven years to writing this book, which I know will take shots from all sides. But I have persisted because I am convinced that the United States is facing both a social and economic crisis—as well as a crucial opportunity. The debate about the value of social programs often involves arguments over who is and is not deserving of government help. This is not a debate I will join. I know we cannot abandon existing residual social policies, policies like welfare, food stamps (Supplemental Nutrition Assistance Program), housing support, etc. In fact, I have not called for that.

For me, the most important discussion is whether social programs actually help people. I am convinced that we must stop believing that social and economic problems can be solved by creating new residual social policies or piling money onto existing programs that do not work. To this day, when I attend academic conferences and think tank meetings, the bottom line of nearly every report, discussion, or white paper is that the government should spend more money. The calls for more money and more residual programs are naive. First and last, *there is no more money.* The federal government has run up an intolerable deficit fighting two wars abroad and coping with financial meltdowns at home. There is presently little public or political will to raise taxes to offset budget deficits. Most 2011 state budgets are disasters, and the true train wreck came on June 30, 2011, when the ARRA (American Recovery and Reinvestment Act) federal funds were exhausted. The obvious second point needs little repeating—*there is no evidence that more money for residual programs will work.*

We have reached the point when no additional investments in residual programs will cure our economic and social problems. Right now the economy is mired in high unemployment and little job creation. Programs to prevent mortgage failures have been unsuccessful. Mortgages fail not just because families cannot afford their first mortgage, but also because their middle-class lifestyles are dependent on drawing money from home equity loans. Many, if not most, mortgage failures cannot be addressed by remedying problems with the first mortgage, because the assets and debts of a single property are tied up in a complex web of first mortgages and home equity debts. People could not afford the homes they bought, many still cannot afford homeownership, and the consumer spending that spins off home ownership is either going to be bogged down or will be fed by another cycle of people taking on debt they cannot afford to pay back.

In the years ahead, those without advanced educational skills will find themselves unemployed, serially unemployed, or stuck at jobs that will never pay more than minimum wage. Employers want more than a degree, they need to hire people with the latest digital and technical skills and analytic abilities.

Instead of discussing the crises, we should focus on the opportunities. I believe that this is a moment for a game-changing social policy. I began the thought experiment that led to this book by considering how to develop a social policy to help disadvantaged children, one that could generate enough support to actually be enacted into law. In the end, I came to one major conclusion: *a residual targeted policy that would genuinely help disadvantaged children is not possible.*

Why did I reach this conclusion? During the time I reviewed the configurations of current social policies, the federal government opted to take on problems of national security and economic stability with policies that have truly mortgaged all children's futures. The national debt has exploded from $5 trillion in 2000 to $14 trillion in March 2011. It is a sad reality that our children and grandchildren will be burdened with the most unmanageable mortgage of all, as they struggle to pay back the enormous debt we have created in the last ten years. More residual social policies would merely increase the size of that mortgage.

As I write the final paragraphs of this book, in July 2011, the economic signs are mixed. The unemployment rate has declined to under 9 percent, but there is still not a widespread housing recovery or job creation. Both federal and state legislatures continue to debate significant budget cuts. Many social advocates are outraged about the proposed cuts in social programs, while some, such as filmmaker Michael Moore, have even gone so far as to claim there is no budget crisis.

In some ways those who dispute the claim that "there is no money" are right. In a speech to protestors demonstrating against Wisconsin Governor Scott Walker's attempts to curtail collective bargaining, Moore proclaimed that America is not broke, that it is in fact "awash in wealth and cash," but the money is only in the hands of the superrich. Moore misdirects his anger. Government also has money. Even without raising taxes, government has the opportunity to create and fund new programs—but that would require abandoning or severely reducing funding for programs and policies that fail to meaningfully help those at whom they are targeted. I could say that I am risking rocking the liberal boat in which I have sailed for much of my career (a more appropriate metaphor is that I risk having my liberal colleagues fire torpedoes at my current boat), but I must contend that some of the proposed budget cuts are in fact appropriate, given that we have so little evidence that the programs targeted for extinction are actually effective. For example, as we have seen, programs like Head Start or funding under the Individuals with Disabilities Education Act have been shown to have little long-term educational benefits despite their widespread popularity. The steady stream of money allocated year after year would better be deployed for the "children's future voucher account" I have proposed (see Chapter 5).

Instead of dithering over the immorality of cutting social programs that feel good but have no major helping impact, I believe that the current economic crisis and political jockeying provide an ideal moment to implement a promising program that can invest in, rather than mortgage, children's futures. I believe that we must draw on our good sense as citizens and muster the will to give every American child the option to be able, upon reaching adulthood, to afford either higher education or homeownership.

This is the moment. We have the opportunity to create and fund a policy that will provide a real future for *all* American children and to invest in sustaining and growing the American middle class. A strong middle class that can afford a middle-class lifestyle without credit card and mortgage debt is the backbone of a great society. We should not allow this opportunity to pass us by.

Endnotes

Chapter 1

1. The term "personal trouble" is drawn from the work of C. Wright Mills, *The Sociological Imagination* (New York: Oxford University Press, 1959). Mills distinguishes between the personal problems experienced by individuals and the "public issues" that transcend the individual and local environments (p. 8). For Mills, a bad marriage would be a personal trouble, while a rising divorce rate would be a public issue.
2. Neil Gilbert and Paul Terrell, *Dimensions of Social Welfare Policies,* 7th ed. (Boston: Allyn & Bacon, 2010).
3. Andrew W. Doblestein, *Social Welfare Policy and Analysis*, 2nd ed. (Chicago: Nelson Hall, 1996).
4. Harold Wilensky and Charles Libeaux, *Industrial Society and Social Welfare* (New York: Free Press, 1968).
5. Section 504 of IDEA requires states to provide children with disabilities a "free and appropriate education" that emphasizes special education and related services to meet the children's unique needs.
6. Title XX, Chapter 33, Subchapter 1, Section 1401:

   (3) Child with a disability

   (A) In general

   The term "child with a disability" means a child—

   (i) with mental retardation, hearing impairments (including deafness), speech or language impairments, visual impairments (including blindness), serious emotional disturbance (hereinafter referred to as "emotional disturbance"), orthopedic impairments, autism, traumatic brain injury, other health impairments, or specific learning disabilities; and

(ii) who, by reason thereof, needs special education and related services.

(B) Child aged 3 through 9

The term "child with a disability" for a child aged 3 through 9 may, at the discretion of the State and the local educational agency, include a child—

(i) experiencing developmental delays, as defined by the State and as measured by appropriate diagnostic instruments and procedures, in one or more of the following areas: physical development, cognitive development, communication development, social or emotional development, or adaptive development; and

(ii) who, by reason thereof, needs special education and related services.

7. Section 794. Nondiscrimination under Federal grants and programs:

(A) Promulgation of rules and regulations

No otherwise qualified individual with a disability in the United States, as defined in section 705 (20) of this title, shall, solely by reason of his or her disability, be excluded from the participation in, be denied the benefits of, or be subjected to discrimination under any program or activity receiving Federal financial assistance or under any program or activity conducted by any Executive agency or by the United States Postal Service. The head of each such agency shall promulgate such regulations as may be necessary to carry out the amendments to this section made by the Rehabilitation, Comprehensive Services, and Development Disabilities Act of 1978. Copies of any proposed regulations shall be submitted to appropriate authorizing committees of the Congress, and such regulation may take effect no earlier than the thirtieth day after the date of which such regulation is so submitted to such committees.

Section 706 (8):

(B) Subject to the second sentence of this subparagraph, the term "handicapped individual" means, for purposes of subchapters IV and V of this chapter, any person who

(i) has a physical or mental impairment which substantially limits one or more of such person's major life activities,

(ii) has a record of such impairment, or

(iii) is regarded as having such an impairment.

8. Special education due process hearings exist in all states. The hearings are a less formal version of a civil trial. In Hawaii, the hearings were held before hearing officers.
9. David Gil, *Violence against Children: Physical Child Abuse in the United States* (Cambridge, MA: Harvard University Press, 1970).
10. C. Henry Kempe, Frederick N. Silverman, Brandt F. Steele, William Droegemueller, and Henry K. Silver, "The Battered Child Syndrome," *Journal of the American Medical Association*, 181 (1962): 17–24.
11. David Cole and Betsy Cole, "Viewpoint: Take a Close Look at Special Ed Costs," *Narragansett Times*, March 29, 2002.

Chapter 2

1. On March 29, 2005, The Brown Schools Inc., an Austin-based operator of schools for troubled youths, filed for Chapter 7 liquidation in the bankruptcy court in Delaware.
2. That percentage remained essentially unchanged in 2008 at 17.74 percent.
3. By 2006 admissions were 150 per year. The service menu remained the same.
4. *Honolulu Star Advertiser*, December 15, 2010, http://www.staradvertiser.com/news/20101215_Jennifer_Felix_now_37_finally_happy_and_stable.html.
5. *Honolulu Star Advertiser*. December 13, 2010, http://www.staradvertiser.com/news/hawaiinews/20101213_Big_gains_not_enough.html.
6. Ibid.

Chapter 3

1. Pub.L. 88-452, 78 Stat. 508, 42 U.S.C. §2701.
2. The local Head Start agency may select what is referred to as "over income" children. If all children below the poverty line are served by the local Head Start program, the program may enroll up to

35 percent of its population with children who come from families between the poverty line and 130 percent of the poverty line.

3. http://www.acf.hhs.gov/programs/opre/hs/eval_hs_fam/eval_hsfam_overview.html.

4. Steven Levitt and Stephen Dubner, *Freakonomics: A Rogue Economist Explores the Hidden Side of Everything* (New York: HarperCollins, 2005).

5. http://papers.ssrn.com/sol3/papers.cfm?abstract_id = 538442.

6. http://www.acf.hhs.gov/programs/opre/hs/impact_study/reports/first_yr_execsum/first_yr_execsum.pdf.

7. The EITC was enacted in 1975 as part of the Tax Reduction Act of 1975 (PL 94-12) and then extended for 1976 in the Tax Revenue Adjustment Act of 1975 (PL 94-164).

8. Alice K. Butterfield, Cynthia J. Rocha, and William H. Butterfield, *The Dynamics of Family Policy Analysis and Advocacy* (Chicago: Lyceum Books, 2010).

9. http://www.taxpolicycenter.org/briefing-book/key-elements/family/eitc.cfm.

10. Center on Budget and Policy Priorities, http://www.cbpp.org/research/index.cfm?fa = topic&id = 27.

11. Butterfield et al., *The Dynamics of Family Policy Analysis and Advocacy*.

12. The 2010 American Recovery and Reinvestment Act included an additional benefit for eligible workers with three or more children. At the end of the 2010 Congressional session, Congress included some revisions to the EITC as part of the extension of unemployment benefits and the Bush-era tax cuts. The final changes were not complete at the time I finished this chapter.

13. http://www.cbpp.org/research/index.cfm?fa = topic&id = 27.

14. http://www.hoover.org/research/factsonpolicy/facts/9199657.html.

15. Ron Haskins, *Work Over Welfare: The Inside Story of the 1996 Welfare Reform Law* (Washington, DC: Brookings Institution Press, 2006).

16. http://www.census.gov/Press-Release/www/2002/cb02-77.html.

17. http://frwebgate.access.gpo.gov/cgi-bin/getdoc.cgi?dbname = 108_green_book&docid = f:wm006_07.pdf.

18. http://www.acf.hhs.gov/programs/ofa/data-reports/caseload/caseload_recent.html.

19. Ibid.

20. Ibid.

21. http://frwebgate.access.gpo.gov/cgi-bin/getdoc.cgi?dbname = 108_green_book&docid = f:wm006_07.pdf.

22. http://www.childtrendsdatabank.org/indicators/75UnmarriedBirths. cfm.
23. http://www.childtrendsdatabank.org/figures/13-figure-1.gif.
24. http://www.acf.hhs.gov/programs/ofa/data-reports/caseload/ caseload_recent.html.
25. June Axinn and Mark Stern, *Social Welfare: A History of the American Response to Need*, 6th ed. (Boston: Pearson, 2005).
26. See for example Axinn and Stern, *Social Welfare*.
27. Social Security Act, Public Law 271, 74th Congress, 1st Session.
28. http://www.ssa.gov/pressoffice/colafacts.htm.
29. http://www.ssa.gov/policy/docs/quickfacts/stat_snapshot/.
30. http://www.census.gov/hhes/www/poverty/data/incpovhlth/2009/ pov09fig04.pdf.
31. http://www.brookings.edu/testimony/2006/0406macroeconomics_ bosworth.aspx.
32. Howard J. Karger and David Stoesz, *American Social Welfare Policy: A Pluralistic Approach*, 4th ed. (Boston: Allyn and Bacon, 2002).
33. Daniel Mitchell, "Creating a Better Social Security System for America," *Backgrounder* #1109 (Washington, DC: The Heritage Foundation, 1997).
34. Ibid.
35. Walt Duka, "A Lot Is at Stake: Bush, Gore Collide over Social Security's Future," *AARP Bulletin*, 41 (September 2000).
36. http://www.ontheissues.org/celeb/al_gore_social_security.htm.
37. Michael Harrington, *The Other America: Poverty in the United States* (New York: Macmillan, 1962).
38. Karger and Stoesz, *American Social Welfare Policy*.
39. http://www.census.gov/prod/2009pubs/p60-236.pdf.
40. http://www.cbpp.org/cms/index.cfm?fa = view&id = 824.
41. Kaiser Family Foundation, *Complete Medicare Fact Sheet*, www.kff. org/medicare/upload/7305.
42. Ibid.
43. http://www.ssa.gov/OACT/TRSUM/index.html.
44. Ibid.
45. Ibid.
46. Axinn and Stern, *Social Welfare*.
47. Edward Humes, *Over Here: How the G.I. Bill Transformed the American Dream* (New York: Harcourt, 2006).
48. Michael J. Bennett, *When Dreams Came True: The GI Bill and the Making of Modern America* (Washington, DC: Brassey's, 1996).

49. Humes, *Over Here*, 32.
50. http://www.gibill.va.gov/GI_Bill_Info/history.htm.
51. Bennett, *When Dreams Came True*, 201.
52. Ibid.
53. James Wright, "The New GI Bill: It's a Win-Win Proposition," *The Chronicle of Higher Education*, May 16, 2008.
54. Bennett, *When Dreams Came True*.
55. Humes, *Over Here*.
56. Arlene S. Skolnick, *Embattled Paradise: The American Family in an Age of Uncertainty* (New York: Basic Books, 1991).

Chapter 4

1. Letter to Robert Hooke (15 February 1676).
2. Irvin Garfinkel and Sara McLanahan, *Single Mothers and Their Children: A New American Dilemma* (Washington, DC: Urban Institute Press, 1986).
3. http://www.vicepresidentdanquayle.com/speeches_StandingFirm_ CCC_1.html.
4. Lindsey, Duncan, *The Welfare of Children*, 2nd ed. (New York: Oxford University Press, 2003). The first edition was published in 1996.
5. Ibid., 319.
6. Bruce Ackermann and Anne Alstott, *The Stakeholder Society* (New Haven: Yale University Press, 1999).
7. Lindsey, Duncan, *Child Poverty and Inequality: Securing a Better Future for America's Children* (New York: Oxford University Press, 2008).
8. http://abcnews.go.com/Politics/story?id = 3668781.
9. Michael Sherraden, *Assets and the Poor: A New American Welfare Policy* (Armonk, NY: M.E. Sharp, 1991).
10. Amitai Etzioni, *The Spirit of Community: Rights, Responsibilities and the Communitarian Agenda* (New York: Crown Publishers, 1993).
11. Amitai Etzioni, *The New Golden Rule: Community and Morality in a Democratic Society* (New York: Basic Books, 1996).
12. Amitai Etzioni, "The Fair Society," in Norton Barfinkle and Daniel Yakelovich, eds., *Uniting America: Restoring the Vital Center to American Democracy* (New Haven: Yale University Press, 2005), 211–223.

13. Amitai Etzioni, "Values and the Future of American Politics," *Contemporary Sociology* 35 (2006): 337–340.
14. Etzioni, "The Fair Society."
15. "Overview of Research into Child Abuse." Testimony before the Committee on Science and Technology, United States House of Representatives, February 16, 1978.
16. U.S. Congress, Joint Hearing before the Subcommittee on Employment, Manpower and Poverty and the Subcommittee on Children and Youth of the Committee on Labor and Public Welfare. United States Senate, on S-1512, Vols. I, II, and III (Washington, DC: Government Printing Office, 1971).
17. See Edward F. Zigler and Susan Muenchow, *Head Start: The History of America's Most Successful Educational Program* (New York: Basic Books, 1992).
18. Kimberly Morgan, "A Child of the Sixties: The Great Society, the New Right, and the Politics of Federal Child Care," *Journal of Policy History* 13 (2001): 215.
19. James J. Kilpatrick, "Child Development Act: To Sovietize Our Youth," quoted in James Welsh, "Educational Legislation," *Educational Researcher* 1, no. 1 (1972): 11–12.
20. U.S. Census Bureau, Housing and Economic Statistics Division.
21. William G. Domhoff, "Power in America: Wealth, Income, and Power," http://sociology.ucsc.edu/whorulesamerica/power/wealth.html. See also http://blogs.wsj.com/wealth/2010/04/30/top-1-increased-their-share-of-wealth-in-financial-crisis/.
22. Elizabeth Warren, Testimony before the Committee on Banking, Housing and Urban Development of the United States Senate, January 25, 2007.

CHAPTER 5

1. Source: U.S. Census Bureau, Population Division, Interim State Population Projections, 2005.
2. Actually, there will be some carry forward obligation for each cohort of eighteen-year-olds, since it is unlikely that youngsters turning eighteen will allocate all their funds in one year.
3. http://www.census.gov/newsroom/releases/archives/education/cb10-55.html.
4. http://nces.ed.gov/fastfacts/display.asp?id = 16.

5. http://www.americaspromise.org/uploadedFiles/Americas PromiseAlliance/Dropout_Crisis/SWANSONCitiesInCrisis040108. pdf.
6. http://www.thecollegecrusade.org/main/images/docs/ scholarship/2007AffirmationForm.pdf.
7. Qualifying children must first be "children" in the sense of §152(f)(1). The term "children" includes adopted children, children placed for adoption, stepchildren, and foster children. Qualifying children must have the same principal place of abode as the taxpayer for more than one half of the year and must not have provided more than one half of their own support. §152(c)(1). They can include a taxpayer's children, a taxpayer's siblings, half-siblings, or step-siblings, or the descendants of a taxpayer's children, siblings, half-siblings, or step-siblings. §§152(c)(2), (f)(4). They may not have reached the age of Nineteen by the close of the year, unless they are students, in which case they must not have reached the age of Twenty-four, or unless they are permanently and totally disabled. §152(c)(3).
8. To complicate matters, there is a phase out for claiming dependent deductions: the amount that can be claimed as a deduction for exemptions is reduced once the adjusted gross income (AGI) goes above a certain level for a given filing status. These levels are as follows:

Filing Status	AGI Level That Reduces Exemption Amount
Married filing separately	$117,300
Single	156,400
Head of household	195,500
Married filing jointly	234,600
Qualifying widow(er)	234,600

The dollar amount of the exemptions must be reduced by 2 percent for each $2,500, or part of $2,500 ($1,250 for married couples filing separately), that AGI exceeds the amount shown above for a particular filing status. However, this reduction cannot exceed two-thirds of the dollar amount of your exemptions. In other words, each exemption cannot be reduced to less than $1,133. See http://www.irs.gov/publications/p501/ar02.html#d0e2859.
9. http://www.irs.gov/pub/irs-soi/02inrate.pdf.
10. http://www.ed.gov/programs/fpg/funding.html. The amount was increased in the 2009 stimulus package.

11. U.S. Department of Education, Fiscal Year 2009 Budget Summary, February 4, 2008.
12. http://www.missingkids.com/en_US/publications/NC171.pdf.
13. http://www.guidestar.org/FinDocuments//2009/521/328/2009-521328557-0660da99-9.pdf.
14. David Finkelhor, Gerald Hotaling, and Andrea Sedlak, *Missing, Abducted, Runaway, and Throwaway Children in America* (Washington, DC: U.S. Department of Justice, Office of Justice Programs, Office of Juvenile Justice and Delinquency Prevention, 1990).
15. Andrew Hacker and Claudia Dreifus, *Higher Education? How Colleges Are Wasting Our Money and Failing Our Kids—And What We Can Do About It* (New York: Henry Holt, 2010); Charles Murray, "For Most People College Is a Waste of Time," *Wall Street Journal*, August 13, 2010.

CHAPTER 6

1. Richard J. Gelles, *The Book of David: How Preserving Families Can Cost Children's Lives* (New York: Basic Books, 1996).
2. Barbara Nelson, *Making an Issue of Child Abuse: Political Agenda Setting for Social Problems* (Chicago: University of Chicago Press, 1984).
3. The biggest increase after 1998 was for the Department of Education. The hiring of a new superintendent of schools was probably one of the factors that led to the increase, as under the new superintendent the DOE rapidly increased its efforts toward complying with the consent decree.
4. U.S. House of Representatives, Committee on Ways and Means, *Green Book: Background Material and Data on the Programs within the Jurisdiction of the Committee on Ways and Means* (Washington, DC: Committee on Ways and Means, 2004), http://www.whitehouse.gov/sites/default/files/omb/budget/fy2011/assets/spec.pdf.
5. Catherine Wilson, "Judge Scolds Department of Children & Families," *Associated Press*, May 6, 2002.
6. David Wasson, "Missing Child's Records Falsified," *Tampa Tribune*, May 2, 2002.
7. Child Protection Report, June 6, 2002, 94.
8. *The Palm Beach Post*, May 29, 2002.
9. U.S. Advisory Board on Child Abuse and Neglect, *Child Abuse and Neglect: Critical First Steps in Response to a National Emergency* (Washington, DC: U.S. Government Printing Office, 1990), 2.
10. CAPTA Reauthorization 2002.

CHAPTER 7

1. Daniel P. Moynihan, *Miles to Go: A Personal History of Social Policy* (Cambridge, MA: Harvard University Press, 1996), 47.
2. Ibid., 48.
3. http://www.mstservices.com/text/treatment.html#glance.
4. Alison Cunningham, *One Step Forward: Lessons Learned from a Randomized Study of Multisystemic Therapy in Canada* (London, Ontario: Center for Children and Families in the Justice System, 2002).
5. Gelles, *The Book of David.*
6. Lawrence W. Sherman and Richard A. Berk, "The Specific Deterrent Effects of Arrest for Domestic Assault," *American Sociological Review* 49 (1984): 261–272.
7. Lawrence W. Sherman, *Policing Domestic Violence: Experiments and Dilemmas* (New York: Free Press, 1992).
8. Darrell Huff, *How to Lie with Statistics* (New York: Norton, 1954).
9. Writing Group for the Women's Health Initiative Investigators, "Risks and Benefits of Estrogen plus Progestin in Healthy Postmenopausal Women," *Journal of the American Medical Association* 288 (2002): 321–333.
10. The 5.2 is an average because the study recruited women over a period of time, but stopped in 2002; thus every woman was not in the study for exactly the same time.
11. Peter Rossi, "Assessing Family Preservation Programs," *Children and Youth Services Review* 14 (1992): 167–191.
12. David L. Olds, John Eckenrode, Charles R. Henderson, Jr. et al., "Long-term Effects of Home Visitation on Maternal Life Course and Child Abuse and Neglect: Fifteen-Year Follow-Up of a Randomized Trial," *Journal of the American Medical Association* 278 (1997): 637–648.

CHAPTER 8

1. There never was a public explanation of why Ransom-Garner resigned but McGee was fired. My best assumption was that both would have been fired, but the difference was due to access to pension benefits.

Index

About the Author

Richard J. Gelles serves as the dean of the School of Social Policy & Practice at the University of Pennsylvania and holds The Joanne and Raymond Welsh Chair of Child Welfare and Family Violence. He is a co-faculty director of the Field Center for Children's Policy, Practice, and Research. In addition, he was the founding director of the Evelyn Jacobs Ortner Center on Family Violence.

His book *The Violent Home* was the first systematic empirical investigation of family violence, and continues to be highly influential. He is the author or coauthor of twenty-four books and more than two hundred articles and chapters on family violence. His latest books are *The Book of David: How Preserving Families Can Cost Children's Lives* (Basic Books, 1996), *Intimate Violence in Families*, 3rd edition (Sage Publications, 1997), and *Current Controversies on Family Violence*, 2nd edition (with Donilene Loseke and Mary Cavanaugh, Sage Publications, 2005).

Gelles received an AB degree from Bates College (1968), an MA in Sociology from the University of Rochester (1971), and a PhD in Sociology from the University of New Hampshire (1973). He edited the journal *Teaching Sociology* from 1973 to 1981 and received the American Sociological Association, Section on Undergraduate Education, Outstanding Contributions to Teaching award in 1979. In 1999 Gelles received the Award for Career Achievement in Research from the American Professional Society on the Abuse of Children. Gelles has presented innumerable lectures to policymaking groups and media groups, including *The Today Show*, *CBS Morning News*, *Good Morning America*, *The Oprah Winfrey Show*, *Dateline*, and *All Things Considered*. In 1984 *Esquire* named him one of the men and women who are changing America.

Presently, Gelles lives in Philadelphia with his wife Judy, a photographer. His son Jason graduated Harvard University in 1996 and is an Emmy Award-winning writer and producer for *The Ellen DeGeneres Show*. His son David graduated Tufts University in 1999 and is an Emmy Award-winning producer for NBC News.

green press

INITIATIVE

Left Coast Press is committed to preserving ancient forests and natural resources. We elected to print this title on 30% post consumer recycled paper, processed chlorine free. As a result, for this printing, we have saved:

2 Trees (40' tall and 6-8" diameter)
1 Million BTUs of Total Energy
195 Pounds of Greenhouse Gases
876 Gallons of Wastewater
56 Pounds of Solid Waste

Left Coast Press made this paper choice because our printer, Thomson-Shore, Inc., is a member of Green Press Initiative, a nonprofit program dedicated to supporting authors, publishers, and suppliers in their efforts to reduce their use of fiber obtained from endangered forests.

For more information, visit www.greenpressinitiative.org

Environmental impact estimates were made using the Environmental Defense Paper Calculator. For more information visit: www.papercalculator.org.